European
Musical Instruments
in
Liverpool Museum

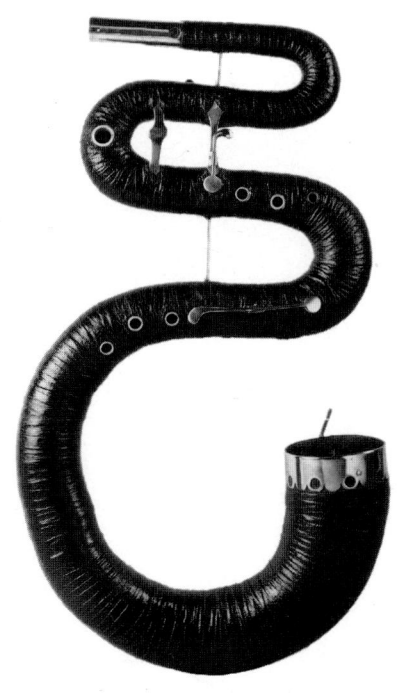

Catalogue of European Musical Instruments

in

Liverpool Museum

PAULINE RUSHTON

National Museums & Galleries
· on Merseyside ·

First published in the United Kingdom in 1994 by the Trustees of the National Museums and Galleries on Merseyside

Copyright © Trustees of the National Museums and Galleries on Merseyside 1994

All rights reserved. No part of this publication may be reproduced, stored in a retrieval system, or transmitted, in any form, or by any means, electronic, mechanical, photocopying, recording or otherwise, without the prior permission of the publishers and copyright holders.

British Library Cataloguing in Publication Data available.

ISBN 0 906367 68 9

Cover illustration: Chamber organ, John Snetzler, London, 1767.

Produced by Alan Sutton Publishing Limited,
Phoenix Mill, Far Thrupp, Stroud, Gloucestershire.
Printed and bound in Great Britain by
Butler & Tanner Ltd, Frome and London

CONTENTS

Foreword		vi
Acknowledgements		viii
Introduction		ix
1.	Keyboard Instruments	1
2.	Organs	45
3.	Free Reed Instruments	59
4.	Wind Instruments	71
5.	Stringed Instruments	107
6.	Percussion Instruments	149
7.	Mechanical Instruments	153
Bibliography		179
Index of makers and retailers		181

Colour plate section between pages 70 and 71

Foreword

The National Museums and Galleries on Merseyside possess one of the largest museum collections of historic musical instruments in Britain. This is in great measure due to William Rushworth of the Liverpool firm of Rushworth and Dreaper Ltd. Between the Wars he built up a corporate collection intended for public benefit, in the best Liverpool tradition of educational philanthropy.

Rushworth was a pioneer in the appreciation of early instruments, at a time when it was still regarded as eccentric, even shocking, to play Bach on a harpsichord rather than a piano. The instruments in his collection were ambassadors for a change of attitude. In restoring some to playing condition he was attempting to enable people to experience – even to re-create for themselves – something of the sound of the past.

Since that time, the change of attitude for which he strove has taken place. The purchase of his collection by the Liverpool Museum in 1967 coincided with the beginning of the most dynamic phase of this revolution in musical ideas.

What is required from a museum collection of historic instruments is now quite different. The sound of everything from virginals to serpent may be heard on record or live in concert. When, for example, a harpsichord is put in playing condition it means subjecting its ancient frame to the strain of one ton or more, an act which is neither prudent nor necessary as excellent modern makers of early instruments of all types now exist. They are interlinked with a whole network of musicians and musicologists. The prime need is for accurate information about the historic instruments surviving in collections. The report *Museums of Music*, commissioned by the Museums and Galleries Commission and published in 1993, emphasised that the most useful such instruments are not those in playing condition but those where restoration has not destroyed evidence of the original state of the instrument. To alter an instrument further from its original condition is to destroy valuable, even vital, evidence.

This collection of historic instruments is therefore maintained as a study collection, available by appointment for examination by researchers and students. This catalogue serves as a guide and introduction, fulfilling the aim of the Trustees of the National Museums and Galleries on Merseyside to publish the collections in its care. Periodic displays of parts of the collection, such as the exhibition *Good Vibrations ! Four Centuries of Music-Making in Europe* held at Liverpool Museum in 1993, interpret the instruments to a broad public. In the longer term, it is hoped to place some of the collection on display on a more permanent basis.

We would like to thank all the specialists who have so generously given their time and expertise to contribute to the catalogue. They are individually named in the acknowledgements. Finally, we owe a special debt of gratitude to Pauline Rushton who has edited the outside contributions, written many of the catalogue entries herself and organised the whole project with efficiency and enthusiasm.

Richard Foster
Director – National Museums and Galleries on Merseyside
Julian Treuherz
Keeper of Art Galleries

Acknowledgements

The editor would like to thank the many people, both colleagues and experts in the field of musical instruments, who have contributed to this publication.

The present board of Rushworth and Dreaper Ltd, in particular Alastair and David Rushworth, have been generous with information and in providing access to the firm's archives.

Thanks go to those who have produced whole entries for the catalogue: Thomas Wess; David Hunt; Dr Alan Barnes; Michael Latcham, Keeper of Musical Instruments at the Gemeentemuseum, The Hague; Andrew Garrett, adviser on musical instruments to the National Trust; and John Griffiths, Curator of Horology, National Museums and Galleries on Merseyside and Curator of Prescot Museum. Their names appear under the particular entries for which they were largely responsible.

Special thanks go to David Hunt for preparing all of the technical specifications for the keyboard instruments and for proof-reading.

The editor is also grateful to the following who have proof-read and corrected the text: Denzil Wraight (virginals); John Barnes and Koen Vermeij (clavichord); Eric Moulder (woodwind instruments); Anne Moore, Curator of the Morpeth Chantry Bagpipe Museum (bagpipes and hurdy-gurdy); Andrew Lamb, Conservator, The Horniman Museum (brass instruments); Dr Frances Palmer, Keeper of Musical Instruments, The Horniman Museum (stringed instruments); and John Griffiths (mechanical instruments).

Much valuable information about the instruments has been discovered during the course of conservation, and the following are thanked for their contributions in this area: Stephen Barber (stringed instruments); David Hunt (keyboard instruments and Bottle Organ); Simon Capp (harps); Tony Smith (balalaikas, zithers, dulcimer); Peter Stanley (banjo); Dave Shaw (Robertson bagpipes); Frank Readey (double bass); Sheila Walthew (virginals); and Jim Hannah (Bremond musical box).

Finally, the editor is indebted to several colleagues in particular for their help with this publication. Dr Angus Gunn, Curator of Extra-European Herbaria in NMGM's Botany Department, checked or identified many of the woods and veneers used in the instruments. David Flower and Clare Bates were responsible for the excellent photographs. Dr Piotr Bienkowski and Robin Emmerson proof-read the text and made many helpful comments.

Pauline Rushton

INTRODUCTION

1. About the collection

The core of Liverpool Museum's collection of European musical instruments is the Rushworth and Dreaper Collection, formed during the 1920s by the Liverpool firm of organ builders and musical-instrument retailers, Rushworth and Dreaper Ltd. The Museum purchased this collection in 1967.

Rushworth's was founded in 1838 by William Rushworth, an organ builder, whose family had moved to Liverpool from Yorkshire during the early years of the nineteenth century. In the 1840s and 1850s he had workshop premises at a number of city-centre addresses before settling at a site in Liverpool's Islington district in 1857.

After William's death, his son, Walter Rushworth, continued the organ-building business, while Walter's brother Edwin opened a shop in front of the Islington organ works, selling pianos and sheet music.

In 1902, the second William Rushworth, Edwin's son, took over the piano-making firm of W.H. and G.H. Draper, which had been established in Bold Street, Liverpool, since 1828. The firm then became known as Rushworth and Dreaper, although there was never actually a Dreaper involved in the business since both Dreaper brothers had died before the takeover, William Henry in 1894 and George Henry in 1895.

In 1911, William Rushworth took over his cousins', Harry and Maynard Rushworths', organ-building part of the family business which had already, in 1908, moved from the Islington premises to a former shawl warehouse in Great George Street, Liverpool. This takeover united the two branches of the firm, instrument making and retailing, for the first time.

The organ works, on which the business was built, developed steadily over the years. During the 1920s, new branches were established in London, Edinburgh and Bristol. By the 1950s, Rushworths had also absorbed a number of other smaller organ-building businesses and instrument retailers. Their main premises in Islington, known as the Rushworth Music House, sold a wide range of pianos, organs and other musical instruments. It housed a lecture theatre and the Rushworth Hall, built in 1910, where musical competitions and regular concerts and recitals by leading musicians were held.

In 1960 the Islington premises were demolished to make way for road development and the business moved to Whitechapel, Liverpool, to the site it still occupies today. In 1974, the Great George Street premises were also demolished and the organ-building works moved to its present location in St Anne Street, Liverpool.

Today, the business is run by the fifth generation of Rushworths and is Liverpool's only remaining family-run firm of instrument makers and retailers.

The Rushworth and Dreaper Collection was largely formed during the 1920s by the second William Rushworth (1870–1944). He was particularly interested in early keyboard instruments and the collection is particularly strong in this area. William adopted an active collecting policy, sending senior staff out on collecting trips around Britain and Europe in search of suitable pieces. Rushworths' archives do not give a complete picture of his collecting activities but they include sufficient detail for us to know that he purchased instruments from several sources: from dealers, private individuals, other collectors, notably the Dutch collector Paul de Wit, and even over the counter in the Islington premises.

Apart from his own personal interest in old instruments, William Rushworth's purpose in collecting was twofold: the collection was to be used for educational and publicity purposes. Once acquired, new pieces were, whenever possible, restored to playing condition and were placed on display in a special gallery in the Rushworth Music House. They were visited and played by music students, school parties and professional musicians alike and also featured in publicity photographs and radio broadcasts. In this, William Rushworth exhibited a marketing ability and an awareness of the educational value of the collection far ahead of his time.

Two catalogues of the collection were published during the period of its display in Islington. Both of them are, unfortunately, undated, but, judging by style and content, *The Rushworth and Dreaper Collection of Antique Musical Instruments and Historical Manuscripts*, with photographs of many of the instruments, probably dates from the 1930s. *The Rushworth and Dreaper Permanent Collection of Antique Musical Instruments*, with line drawings and in at least two editions, probably dates from the 1940s or early 1950s. They are referred to in this publication as R & D catalogue 1 and R & D catalogue 2.

Since 1967, when Liverpool Museum purchased the Rushworth and Dreaper Collection, other instruments, particularly those with a Liverpool connection, have been added to it. Today, the Rushworth and Dreaper material forms approximately half of the Museum's entire collection of European musical instruments.

2. About the catalogue

This catalogue of the collection is divided into sections for each main type of instrument. Within each individual section similar instruments are grouped together and arranged chronologically. Where a technical specification has been included, this refers to the current state of the instrument.

Information about makers and retailers has been included wherever possible and has only been omitted where such information was not available. Where it is included, details are given under the first relevant instrument and not subsequently where that maker or retailer may recur in entries for other instruments. Dates given for makers are, as far as possible, those between which they were active under their own name, or, where applicable, until they were absorbed by another firm and ceased to trade under their own name. An index of makers and retailers is included at the back of the catalogue.

Pauline Rushton

Keyboard Instruments

1.1. VIRGINALS, attributed to Francesco Poggi, Florence, c.1610–1620

Museum Accession Number 1967.161.13

TECHNICAL SPECIFICATION

Inscription	*Joannes Antonius Baffo* *Venetus F MDLXXXI* (spurious)
Soundboard Signature	*Arnold Dolmetsch 1895*
Lid Signature	*Io (?) Del Marchese Ipollito Bondelmonte*
Nameboard Inscription	*Pesario* (on rear)
Present Compass	4 Octaves and a fourth, C – f^3. Chromatic – 54 notes
Original Compass	C/E – f^3. Broken bass octave, 6 split sharps – 56 notes
3-Octave-Span	488 mm. Ebony naturals, boxwood sharps
Stringing	1 x 8 foot

	C	c^2	f^3
Scaling	1466mm	329mm	121mm
Pluck-Point	270mm	94mm	65mm
Gauges Extant	–	0.38mm	–

Action	Single manual. Single register of jacks
Inner Case Size	Length 1613mm, Width 440mm, Depth 217mm
Outer Case Size	Length 1675mm, Width 485mm, Depth 257mm
Maker	Francesco Poggi, active *c.*1586–*c.*1634

DESCRIPTION

As is usual with Italian virginals, this instrument is housed in an outer case from which it can be removed. The centre of the outer surface of the lid has been painted with an armorial coat-of-arms, surrounded by scrolling vegetation, in a number of coloured pigments. The entire surface of the outer case has then been covered with a dark red-coloured pigment or stain. The inner surface of the lid has been crudely painted with 10 figures, dressed in 'Classical' costume. The central group of four female figures is grouped around a harpsichord. Three of them are standing, playing a recorder (?), a violin and a lute. The fourth figure is seated at the keyboard, writing with a quill pen. They are flanked by two male figures on the left-hand side and four on the right-hand side, observing them play. The outer case is probably of a later date than the rest of the instrument, and the painting on the underside of the lid, at least, is crude and appears to have been executed during the nineteenth century.

The inner case is made from cypress wood. The inside lip of the case is decorated with scrolling, gold-coloured leaves and flowers, painted on a black ground, the paint being limited to the areas which could be seen when the instrument was placed in the outer case. This was common Italian practice and indicates that the instrument was not removed from the outer case during normal use. Similarly, the case mouldings are not continued where they would not be seen, for instance on either side of the keywell and along the sides and back. There is a cornice moulding inside the back and sides, decorated with finely painted scrollwork in gold on a black ground, but this does not continue along the front. The cap moulding goes right round the instrument.

The jackrail and triangular-shaped toolbox lid, the latter situated in the top right-hand corner of the soundboard, are both of spruce. The jackrail and the moulded, diagonal edge of the toolbox lid are both decorated with the same wandering pattern of gold leaves and tiny gold scrolls, painted on a black ground, as that found on the inside lip of the case and the inside mouldings. The spurious signature *Baffo* is marked on the toolbox lid.

The panel above the keyboard, and the areas on either side of the keywell, are decorated with finely executed bird paintings, surrounded by borders of delicately painted scrollwork, which can just be seen below the layer of red stain. The carved and painted keycheeks are probably of cypress.

It is possible that the nameboard immediately above the keyboard originally carried the maker's signature on the back, but that this was removed when the nameboard was cut along the bottom edge and small recesses made in it to accommodate the sharps of the present keyboard. The cutting off of the bottom section appears to have been carried out only in order to lower the nameboard and provide new holes for the screws which now hold it in position, the original wooden pegs having been lost.

The keylevers are probably of chestnut; the naturals have ebony covers and the sharps are of boxwood. The keyboard arcades are of ebony and boxwood. The guide rack at the back of the keyframe has a capping piece (with sewing holes to allow felt or cloth to be fitted), to limit keydip during playing. The keydip is now limited by felt fixed under the front ends of the keys (possibly by Arnold Dolmetsch), and an extra piece of wood has been added to limit the dip of the sharps.

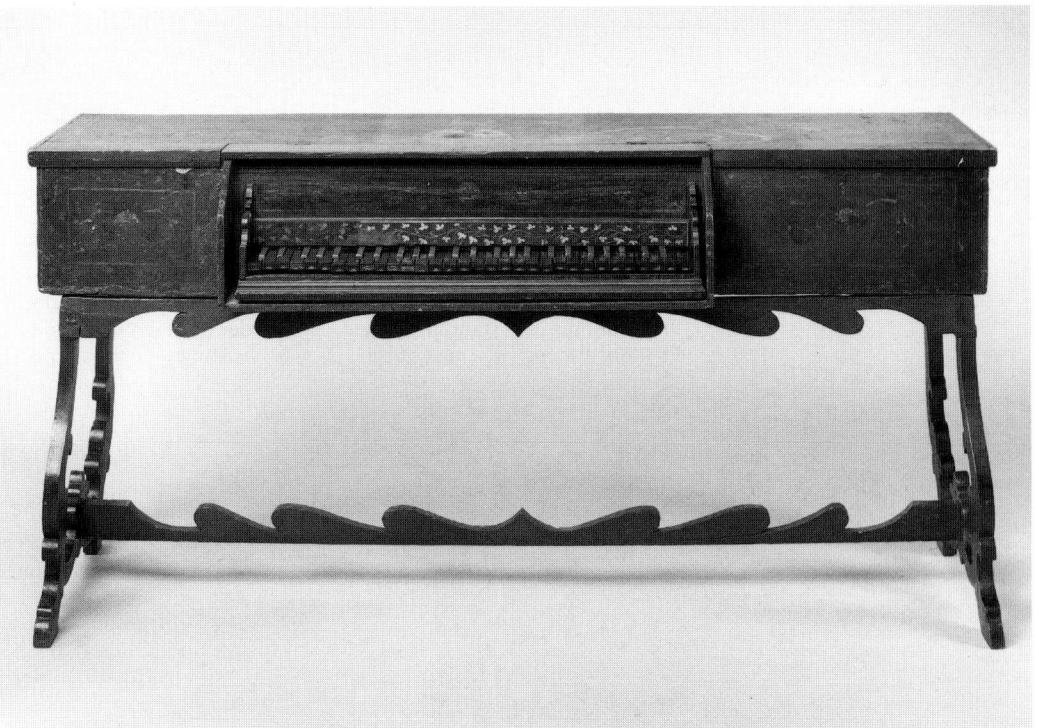

During a detailed examination, Thomas Wess discovered that, although the present keylevers are not original, the keyframe itself is part of the original instrument and that traces of the original balance pins and part of the original guide rack still remain. From these traces it was possible to show that originally the compass was 4 ½ octaves, C/E to f³, and that there were six split sharps; two for the 'broken octave' bass and four for the middle two octaves, to give separate, and therefore better, tunings for d sharp and e flat, and for g sharp and a flat. This gives 56 notes rather than the more usual 45 or 50 notes common during the sixteenth century, and this matches the remains of the guide rack and the slots in the soundboard.

The present keylevers were fitted to the original frame during comprehensive and skillful alterations around 1700. Changes in musical style and the development of more flexible but less pure tuning systems at that time called for a fully chromatic but simpler keyboard. This required only 54 instead of the earlier 56 notes, but did, however, result in an increase in the number of natural keys, and the present keyboard has 33 naturals whereas the original would have had only 30. In order to fill the width of the keywell, the old naturals must have been wider than the present ones and may well have measured about 170mm to the octave. The wide naturals are not uncommon on Italian instruments, but in this case may be the result of the original maker allowing himself enough room on the jackguide to fit 14 jacks into an octave, to accommodate the split sharps, instead of the usual 12.

The soundboard is made from cypress. Originally, it had 56 slots for the jacks but the top two have been plugged because they were not needed for the present compass of 54 notes. The two bridges are of walnut but only the left-hand one is original and this has been shortened by approximately one inch, as part of the alterations of about 1700. The position of the original right-hand bridge, which was removed during the alterations, can be seen quite clearly on the soundboard, and there are several tiny plugged holes in the soundboard which show where the maker placed pins to position the bridge accurately for glueing. Similar holes alongside the left-hand

bridge show that it has not been moved. The present right-hand bridge dates from the alterations of about 1700 and is of a slightly different shape to the original, to allow for the shorter string lengths necessitated by pitch changes. Most of the present strings were probably fitted by Dolmetsch in 1895, but there are others of a more recent date.

On the underside of the soundboard there are two cypress bars, one on either side of the parchment rose, which were fitted by the maker. There are also 10 bars of spruce; two under the right-hand bridge area of the soundboard, two in front of the jackguide towards the left side of the keywell, five under the left-hand bridge, and one under the left side of the soundboard. These were almost certainly fitted by Dolmetsch in 1895, probably to strengthen and flatten the soundboard which was by then showing various cracks and had become depressed due to the pressure of the strings. It would appear that he fitted them by removing the base of the instrument, since removal of the soundboard would have meant damaging the painting on the mouldings and on the inner sides of the case. Dolmetsch's signature and the date 1895 appear on the soundboard to the left of the highest tuning-pin.

The majority of the jacks are Italian and original. The replacements, probably also the work of Dolmetsch, appear to be of close-grained mahogany. All the springs are of pigs-bristle but the Italian jacks would originally have had flat leaf springs. The plectra are now of leather, replacing the original quill.

The painted trestle stand, with lyre-shaped supports, appears to be of a later date, possibly the eighteenth or nineteenth century.

Some features of the alterations of *c*.1700 (black naturals, ebony sharps, chestnut keylevers) might have suggested that the work was carried out in England. However, Denzil Wraight, as a result of his research into moulding sections, has identified the key arcades as those of Cristofori, on the basis that they are identical to the arcades of the 1693 Cristofori spinet (No.53, Musikinstrumenten-Museum, Leipzig). Since the arcades of the 1693 spinet do not appear on any other Cristofori instrument, the modifications to the keyboard would appear to have been carried out before 1720, the date of the next Cristofori instrument, which has different arcades.

Thomas Wess, on the bases of the original keyboard configuration and the decorative style, has suggested that the instrument was made in Tuscany *c*.1610–1620. Denzil Wraight, by comparing the design and execution of the keycheeks with those of another virginals (No.1596, Musee Instrumental, Royal Conservatory, Brussels, which is attributed to the Florentine maker Poggi), suggests that this instrument is almost certainly by the same maker.

Thomas Wess
Denzil Wraight

HISTORY OF THE INSTRUMENT

Provenance   Sir Lawrence Alma-Tadema, –1912
Lord Leverhulme, 1913–1926
Rushworth and Dreaper Ltd, Liverpool, 1926–1967

Details of the early ownership of this instrument are unknown, although sometime during the late nineteenth century it certainly passed through the hands of the well-known faker of early keyboard instruments, Leopoldo Franciolini of Florence (Russell, 1959, p.145).

It is not known how the artist Alma-Tadema came to own the instrument, nor when, but it formed part of his collection until his death in 1912. It was sold, together with all his other effects, on 12th June, 1913, by Hampton and Sons, from his home at number 34 Grove End Road, London. It was lot number 827 in Hampton's catalogue, and was described as being located in 'the Dutch Room and Bedchamber ajoining'.

It was purchased by Gooden and Fox, on behalf of William Hesketh Lever, later the first Viscount Leverhulme, for 150 guineas. Commission at 2 ½% brought the total figure to £161.8.9.

It remained in Leverhulme's collection until his death in 1925. It was sold, with the rest of his collections, on 4th June, 1926, at the Hanover Square galleries of Knight, Frank and Rutley. It appears in their sale catalogue as lot number 278. The entry indicates that it had been kept by Leverhulme at Hulme Hall, at Port Sunlight on the Wirral, where he had displayed his collections before the completion in 1922 of the Lady Lever Art Gallery.

It was purchased by Broadwoods, on behalf of Rushworth and Dreaper, for the sum of £36.15.0.

REFERENCES

R & D catalogue 1 (undated), not paginated.
R & D catalogue 2 (undated), p.4.
Sale catalogue, Hampton and Sons, 1913, p.54, lot 827.
Sale catalogue, Knight, Frank and Rutley, 1926, p. 29, lot 278.
The Liverpolitan, 1937, p.14.
Boalch, 1956, p.4, no.6 (Baffo).
Russell, 1959, pp.35, 145.
Spiegl, 1972, pp.43, 49.
Russell, 1973, p.35.
Boalch, 1974, p.8, no.6 (Baffo).
Whittington-Egan, 1976, p.158.
Taylor, 1976, p.101.
Bevan, 1990, p.68.
Wraight, 1992, p.701.

1.2. SPINET, John Kirshaw, Manchester, *c.*1750–1760

Museum Accession Number 1967.161.8

TECHNICAL SPECIFICATION

Nameboard Inscription	*John Kirshaw Manchester*
Compass	5 Octaves, FF – f^3, no FF#
3-Octave-Span	483mm. Ivory naturals, ebony sharps
Stringing	1 x 8 foot

	FF	c^2	f^3
Scaling	1620mm	359mm	118mm
Strike-Point	172mm	101mm	66mm
Gauges Extant	0.66mm	0.33mm	0.27mm

Action	Single manual. Single register of jacks
Case Size	Length 1902mm, Depth 244mm
Maker	John Kirshaw, active *c.*1740–1773
DESCRIPTION	The wing-shaped case is probably of oak, veneered with panels of burr walnut, crossbanded with walnut and inlaid with a dark and a light wood stringing. The inside lip of the case is also veneered with walnut and inlaid with a dark and a light wood stringing. The top of the lip on the instrument's spine is stamped R & D 30000. The lid is

There are two bridges and two nuts of beech. The wrest plank is of oak, veneered with sycamore. There are two jackrails, both veneered with mahogany, secured on the right-hand side of the case with a brass hook and a brass clip respectively. Both are probably later nineteenth century replacements.

Four handstops, their brass knobs located in pairs above the keyboard on either side, control the four registers of jacks. One of these brass stop-knobs is a modern replacement. A knee-lever for the machine-stop, located below the keyboard on the left-hand side now replaces the original pedal. The oak box for the machine stop mechanism is attached to the spine of the case.

The solid mahogany trestle stand with brass castors is not original and probably dates from the late nineteenth century.

This instrument has distorted very badly in the past. The case has gradually twisted at the tail end, and it was unfortunately planed down in an effort to disguise this, resulting in some loss of cross-banding on the top of the case at that end. The treble cheek is also badly twisted and so the pitch has been lowered to prevent further damage.

HISTORY OF THE INSTRUMENT

Provenance

Dr Edward Hill, Dublin
Mrs Annie Spencer Curwen, 1895–1927
Rushworth and Dreaper Ltd, Liverpool, 1927–1967

It is not known exactly when this instrument was purchased by Dr Edward Hill (1741–1830), nor if he bought it directly from Kirckman himself or from a third party. However, it remained in the Hill/Curwen family, as related in the label attached to the inside of the lid, until 2nd November, 1927, on which date it was purchased from Mrs Annie Spencer Curwen by Rushworth and Dreaper for the sum of £200.

Edward Hill was born in Ballyporeen, Co. Tipperary, in 1741. He was appointed Regius Professor of Physic at Trinity College Dublin in 1781. Between 1782 and 1813, he held the Presidency of the Royal College of Physicians six times. In 1785 he was appointed Professor of Botany at Trinity College. He died in Dublin in 1830.

John Spencer Curwen was the son of John Curwen (1816–1880), a Congregationalist minister, who developed the Tonic Sol-Fa method of sight-singing for choral groups in the 1840s. This method enabled singers to read music without necessarily having to learn the complex system of musical notation.

REFERENCES

R & D catalogue 1 (undated), not paginated.
R & D catalogue 2 (undated), p.5.
The Liverpolitan, 1937, p.15.
Blom, 1954, p.765, no.23.
Boalch, 1956, p.64, no.35.
Boalch, 1974, p.89. no.35.
Bevan, 1990, p.68.

1.4 HARPSICHORD, Burkat Shudi and John Broadwood, London, 1774

Museum Accession Number 1967.161.6

TECHNICAL SPECIFICATION

Serial Number	736
Nameboard Inscription	*Burkat Shudi et Johannes Broadwood No 736 Londini Fecerunt 1774*
Compass	5 Octaves. FF – f^3, no FF#
3-Octave-Span	487mm. Ivory naturals, ebony sharps
Stringing	2 x 8 foot

	FF	c^2	f^3
Scaling	1835/1823mm	347/331mm	131/124mm
	(Longer 8 foot/Shorter 8 foot)		
Pluck-Point	180/195mm	92/105mm	58/72mm
Gauges Extant	0.62mm	0.35mm	0.27mm
Gauges Marked	13	4	4

Action	Single manual, 2 registers of jacks
Stops	2 Handstops: Back 8 foot
	Front 8 foot
Case Size	Length 2298mm, Width 936mm, Depth 295mm
Makers	Burkat Shudi (1702–1773)
	John Broadwood (1732–1812)

DESCRIPTION

The case is of oak, veneered and crossbanded with mahogany and with panels of flame-figured mahogany, and inlaid with maple stringing. The lid is of solid mahogany, secured on the underside with five modern mahogany battens. There are three shaped brass strap hinges on the lid and four brass hinges on each of its two folding front sections. The nameboard is veneered with sycamore. The keyboard surround and keycheeks are also veneered with sycamore, inlaid with maple stringing. The moulded keyfronts are of maple. There are two square panels of satinwood inlaid at either side of the adjustable mahogany music-stand, which is a replacement.

The soundboard is probably of spruce, and the bridge and nut are of beech. The wrest-plank is of oak veneered with mahogany. The jackrail is of spruce veneered with mahogany and inlaid with maple stringing. It is secured at the right-hand side of the case with a brass hook.

Two handstops with brass knobs, one at each side of the keyboard, control the two registers of jacks. The knobs are later replacements. The mahogany trestle stand with wooden castors appears to be original.

HISTORY OF THE INSTRUMENT

Provenance
Charles Avison, 1774 –
T. Andrews and Co., Guildford, Surrey, –1933
Rushworth and Dreaper Ltd, Liverpool, 1933–1967

The Shudi and Broadwood Journal (Bodleian MS. Eng. misc. b.107) records that this instrument was made for Charles Avison in 1774.

This was probably Charles Avison junior (1751–1795), son of the famous musician (c.1710–1770).

It was purchased by Rushworth and Dreaper from T. Andrews and Co., 144 High Street, Guildford, in April 1933 for £60. Andrews and Co., founded by Thomas Andrews at 100 High Street, Guildford in 1857, specialised in the sale of modern and historic pianos. They still continue in business today at Farncomb, Surrey.

REFERENCES Boalch, 1956, p.109.
Boalch, 1974, p.161.
Mould, 1974, p.53.

1.5. CLAVICHORD, Christian Gottlob Hubert, Anspach, 1783

Museum Accession Number 1967.161.11

TECHNICAL SPECIFICATION

Internal Label	*Christian Gottlob Hubert*
	Hoff Instrumenten Bauer fecit
	Andzbach Ao: 1783
Compass	4 Octaves and a fifth, C – g^3
3-Octave-Span	473mm. Ebony naturals, ivory-capped sharps, (3 replacement bone-capped sharps)
Stringing	Bichord, 40 pairs

	C	c^2	g^3
Scaling	1207mm	260mm	74mm
Gauges Extant	0.56mm	0.35mm	0.33mm

Action	Double fretted, except C – e, a, d^1, a^1, d^2, a^2, d^3, g^3
Case Size	Length 1408mm, Width 368mm, Depth 128mm
Maker	Christian Gottlob Hubert (1714–1793)

DESCRIPTION

The case is of pine, veneered and crossbanded on the front and sides with oak and walnut in a herringbone pattern, and inlaid with stringing in a darker wood. The lid is of solid oak, hinged down the length, with both sections divided into three fielded panels. It is secured to the back of the case by two brass hinges and a leather strap on the left-hand side. The front section of the lid is attached to the back section by three shaped brass hinges, and there are two brass locks on the keyboard flap.

The top lip of the case is of a fruitwood, probably pear, and appears to have been added at a later date. The rebated inner lip of the case is stained red and there is a strip of paper, printed with blue dots, glued along the back and left-hand side of the lip. This is the same pattern as that found on several other Hubert clavichords, indicating that it is likely to be original, but it is missing from around the soundboard, which may mean that the latter was removed at some point for repair.

The case fits into the top of the stand, which has four fluted, tapering sycamore legs and is also veneered and crossbanded with oak and walnut in a herringbone pattern. There are two narrow drawers in the front of the stand, their fronts veneered with walnut, with cast brass handles, each decorated with a tiny shell motif. One of these handles is a modern reproduction. The bottom lip of the stand is decorated with a band of alternating light and dark wood, probably sycamore and a dark fruitwood, and the corners are carved with overlapping leaf motifs. Underneath, the stand is stencilled twice with a large black *6*, on the base and centre back. Although it appears to match the case, the stand may be a later reconstruction, as maintained by James (1970, p.96), and could date from the late nineteenth century.

The soundboard appears to be of spruce, and the bridge, with scrolled end, is of beech. The strings are attached to the steel hitch pins on an extended, red-stained hitch rail which runs along the back and the left-hand side of the case. There are 80 iron wrest-pins on the right-hand side of the soundboard, their notes marked beside them on two long strips of paper, inserted between the tuning-pins and glued to the soundboard.

The guide pins at the back of the keys are original but the balance pins are modern and were probably replaced as a way of taking up wear in the balance holes.

The removable nameboard of stained cherry bears no signature and appears to be a later replacement. It lacks the mouldings which the original would probably have had. The maker's name is inscribed on a paper label attached to the inner left side of the case. There is also a narrow toolbox on the left-hand side, with a hinged lid.

HISTORY OF THE INSTRUMENT

Provenance Paul de Wit, Leipzig, –1922
Rushworth and Dreaper Ltd, Liverpool, 1922–1967

It is not known where this instrument was located before it came into the possession of Paul de Wit, but a record in the archives of Rushworth and Dreaper states that they purchased it from him on 12th September, 1922 for the sum of £19.13.11.

REFERENCES R & D catalogue 1 (undated), not paginated.
R & D catalogue 2 (undated), p.4.
The Liverpolitan, 1937, pp.14–15.
Boalch, 1956, p.55, no.8.
Russell, 1959, p.106.
Hands, 1967, p.89.
James, 1970, p.96, pl.XVI.
Russell, 1973, p.106.
Boalch, 1974, p.76, no.8.
Taylor, 1976, p.101.
Strack, 1977, pp.1554–1557.
Strack, 1979, pp.54–55., pl XII, no.14.
Bevan, 1990, p.68.

1.6. SQUARE PIANO, Schrader and Hartz, London, c.1795

Museum Accession Number 1967.161.4

TECHNICAL SPECIFICATION

Nameboard Inscription *Schrader and Hartz Successors to Gabriel Buntebart Princes Street / Hanover Square*

Internal Label *Schrader and Hartz, Successors to Gabriel Buntebart Princes Street, Hanover Square, in London, Zeit um 1780–1790, grosse Seltenheit*

Compass 4 Octaves and a fourth, C – f^3

3-Octave-Span 469mm. Ivory naturals, ebony sharps

Stringing Bichord throughout

	C	c^2	f^3
Scaling	945mm	288mm	102mm
Strike-Point	50mm	34mm	17mm
Gauges Extant	0.94mm	0.35mm	0.29mm

Action English single. Overdampers throughout

Stops 1 Handstop – Damper lift

Case Size Length 1056mm, Width 432mm, Depth 176mm

Makers Schrader and Hartz, active together from *c.*1795 (?)

DESCRIPTION The case is of solid mahogany. There is a narrow skirting around the base of the case, also of mahogany. The lid is of solid mahogany, with a hinged front section and hinged keyboard flap. It is attached to the back of the case by two modern brass hinges and the front section is attached to the back section by a further five modern brass hinges. The right-hand side of the front section of the lid opens separately. When the lid is open, the keyboard flap and a lip on the underside of the front section act as a music stand. The lid is supported by a short, pivoted mahogany lid-prop, probably a modern replacement, attached to the inside of the case on the left-hand side. There is a modern lock on the lid which is attached upside down.

The case rests on a plain mahogany stand with moulded stretchers running between front and back legs, strengthened by another horizontal stretcher running between them. The stand appears to be a modern replacement, probably dating from the late 1960s. Early photographs of the instrument show that it previously stood on four tapering, octagonal-shaped legs which screwed into the base of the case and are now missing.

The spruce soundboard and beech bridge are both modern replacements. There is a strip of modern mahogany glued and nailed all around the top edge of the soundboard. The removable pine nameboard, veneered with mahogany, crossbanded with sycamore and inlaid with a darker wood stringing, appears to have been re-written at some point. The keycheeks are also veneered with mahogany, crossbanded with sycamore and inlaid with a darker wood stringing.

There is a modern label attached to the inner right-hand side of the case, marked *Do not raise pitch above Continental – C 517.3*. The strings are modern replacements, as are the 106 steel wrestpins on the right-hand side of the soundboard.

This instrument appears to have lost many of its original features during extensive restoration in the late 1960s.

HISTORY OF THE INSTRUMENT

Provenance Paul de Wit, Leipzig, –1922
Rushworth and Dreaper Ltd, Liverpool,1922–1967

It is not known where this instrument was located before it came into the collection of Paul de Wit in Leipzig. It was purchased from him by Rushworth and Dreaper on the 9th September 1922 and 'cost £14 plus expenses and duty. Total cost – £21.10.0'.

REFERENCES R & D catalogue 1 (undated), not paginated.
R & D catalogue 2 (undated), p.5.
Bevan, 1990, p.68.

1.7. SEWING BOX PIANO, unsigned, south German or Austrian, *c.*1805

Museum Accession Number 1967.161.9

TECHNICAL SPECIFICATION

Inscription None

Compass 2 Octaves and a fifth, $f^2 - c^5$ (at 8 foot pitch)
$f^1 - c^4$ (at 4 foot pitch)

3-Octave-Span 306mm. Ebony naturals, bone-capped sharps

Stringing 8 singles – c^3. Bichord – c^5

	f^2	c^3	c^5
Scaling	173mm	143mm	49mm
Strike-Point	42mm	28mm	9mm
Gauges Extant	0.53mm	0.44mm	0.3mm

Action German escapement action with no check and no dampers

Case Size Length 348mm, Width 244mm, Depth 144mm

DESCRIPTION

The case is made of pine, veneered on the sides with mahogany, and on the top of the lid with sycamore, laid in a geometric pattern, inlaid with ebony stringing and crossbanded with mahogany. The underside of the lid is veneered with plain sycamore. The front flap, veneered with mahogany on the outside and with sycamore on the inside, is now hinged to the main lid but was probably once separate. The string for holding open the lid is not original and there may have been a lid-prop which fitted a slot cut into the main lid on the left-hand side. The inner lip of the case, above a small ledge, is veneered with green stained sycamore, but the area below the ledge is not veneered. The ledge probably once acted as a carrier for a shallow tray. Such trays are often found in miniature pianos of this kind, divided into compartments to hold writing or toilette accessories or sewing equipment. The drawer underneath the action probably served a similar purpose.

The instrument has no stand or legs and would have been used on a table. Around the base of the case is a skirting of green-stained

sycamore, formed at the front by the drawer. The nameboard, which is detachable, slips down into slots in the keyboard end blocks, which are shaped to form handles for pulling the keyboard out to playing position.

On the inside of the back of the case, upside down in pencil, there is an illegible and possibly original inscription.

The soundboard is of spruce, with one large rib and an 'apron'. The bridge is stained black and is probably of walnut. Both the bridge and the nut, also probably of walnut, have or had carved scrolls at each end. Where extensions of the bridge at both its ends would meet the side walls of the case, there are chamfers in the liners. The wrestplank and hitchpin rail, the latter running along the back of the case on top of the soundboard, are both of beech. The wrestplank is veneered with sycamore. There are 56 iron wrestpins. The hitchpins are also of iron and the bridge and nut pins of brass. An iron brace runs between the bellyrail and the wrestplank, beneath the soundboard, to strengthen the construction and help take up the tension of the strings.

The keyboard and action are drawn out of the body of the instrument in order to play it, the drawer beneath acting as a sledge. At the treble end of the keyboard there is the signature *W.J. Parr 17/8/1964* in ink and *1942* in pencil. Beneath the keyboard there is marked *W.J. Parr Repaired 1948*.

The action has wooden kapsels mounted on the keys. The kapsels, the upright pawls, the hammer shanks and the hammer heads are all of lime, and the leather on the hammers has been replaced at some point. The keylevers appear to be of spruce, and have been weighted later by the addition of pearwood blocks glued on top and underneath. The kapsels are set in oak (?) blocks on the keys with iron stems. The pawls were once sprung in the usual way. Their motion is now restricted by a long, horizontal piece of wood, turning what was once a refined escapement action into a simple bumper action. The keys are guided in a rack at the back, and the cover of the rack also serves to limit the upward motion of the keys. The keyframe is of beech.

One unusual feature of this piano is the fact that the strings run from front to back, as on a grand piano, whereas square pianos usually have the strings running from side to side. Some of the strings are certainly old and could be original. Their diameters suggest the Nurnberg gauge system.

This instrument has no dampers, otherwise no essential element of the German piano is lacking from its construction. Michael Latcham, having made a full examination of it, maintains that, despite its size, this piano was built with serious intent and not simply as a toy. The care with which the liners are chamfered for the bridge and the accuracy and detail of the action further prove this. The action has wooden kapsels, upright pawls and no check, the three features which distinguish the German action, made famous by Johann Andreas Stein (1728–1792), from the Viennese. In the Viennese action, there is a check, the pawls lean forward towards the beaks of the hammer shanks, and the kapsels are of brass.

Given that sewing box pianos did not generally come into vogue until about 1800, and the fact that the German action went out of fashion around 1805, Michael Latcham has dated this instrument to *c.*1805, although he points out that it is possible that the tradition of the German action continued after 1805 in provincial instruments or possibly in such small instruments as this one. It has not, however, been possible to attribute it to any particular maker, although it is certainly in the tradition of Stein and his pupils.

Michael Latcham

HISTORY OF THE INSTRUMENT

Provenance

Carl August, Duke of Saxe-Weimar-Eisenach
George Krenke, Dresden, –1929
Rushworth and Dreaper Ltd, Liverpool, 1929–1967

Rushworth and Dreaper purchased this instrument from (the dealer ?) George Krenke of Dresden 'about 9th June, 1929.' The total cost was £4.0.0.

A note in Rushworth and Dreaper's archives states that it had once belonged to the collection of 'Carl August, Duke of Weimar'. This was probably Carl August, Duke, later Grand Duke, of Saxe-Weimar-Eisenach (1757–1828).

REFERENCES

Whittington-Egan, 1976, p.158.

1.8. GRAND PIANO, unsigned, south German or Austrian, c.1810

Museum Accession Number 1967.161.12

TECHNICAL SPECIFICATION

Nameboard Inscription None

Compass 5 Octaves and a fifth, FF – c^4

3-Octave-Span 473mm. Ebony naturals, bone-capped sharps

Stringing Bichord FF – b^1, trichord c^2 – c^4

	FF	c^2	c^4
Scaling	1616mm	295mm	80mm
Strike-Point	147mm	29mm	9mm
Gauges Extant	1.12mm	0.43mm	0.33mm

Action Viennese hammer action with continuous check. Overdampers throughout

Stops 2 Knee-levers: Moderator
                      Damper lift

Case Size Length 1996mm, Width 1067mm, Depth 279mm

DESCRIPTION The sides of the case are of solid sycamore, the bent side made up of two laminations. The lid is also of solid sycamore, with clamps on the end grain sides. The lid has been slightly cut down. The wood probably shrank across the grain and the clamps were cut to match the shrunken width. The keyboard surround and the keycheeks are veneered with sycamore, with a lip of ebony running all around. The keyblocks are ebonised and decorated with gilt acorn-shaped knobs. The four tapering legs are square in section. Around the base of the case there is a stringing let into the wood about 50mm from the bottom, giving the impression of a skirting. Where the legs join the case, this skirting protrudes from the case in square blocks 3mm thick.

The wreath-shaped ormolu mounts on these blocks, and the central scrolling urn design flanked by swan-shaped mounts in the keywell, are probably later additions. Some of them can be found in a Viennese pattern book of the 1820s, *Musterbuch gepresster Metalarbeiten (ornamentalen Charakters) aus der Fabrick der Gebruder Feil in Wien*. The sloping shoulders of the case, either side of the keyboard, are typical of Austrian pianos of the period *c.*1785–1805. Both the lid-prop and the music stand of sycamore are later additions. Two lid hooks are missing and the main lid hinges are later replacements, although most of the small hinges are original.

The baseboard is strengthened underneath by a wide frame glued around the perimeter. The baseboard itself is only visible as a triangle, the long side of which runs from the tail to the front treble corner. Two large knee-levers, probably replacements of older ones, operate a replacement moderator and the dampers.

The soundboard is of spruce and has been cut out for repairs in the recent past, probably during the late 1970s. When it was put back, a new bentside liner appears to have been made. The new liner was glued to the old one rather than replacing it, altering the area of free soundboard. The soundboard and hitchpin rail were both varnished at that time. All the hitchpins, bridge pins, nut pins and wrestpins are

later replacements. The hitchpin rail also appears to have been lowered in the recent past, probably with the intention of improving down-bearing. The strings are all modern replacements.

The bridge is either of pearwood or apple and has been repaired with beech. It is reduced in height at both ends, before entering the spine in the bass and the cheek in the treble. The last section of the bridge in the base, carrying four courses of strings, runs parallel to the tail in the manner of Italian harpsichords. The cross-section of the bridge is a simple rectangle with chamfers on both top corners. All the strings are back-pinned. The wrestplank is of oak with a sycamore veneer. It is situated higher in the case than the soundboard and is strengthened by a yoke consisting of three members, two of which are glued at the sides of the wrestplank and extend over the gap to the soundboard. The third, which joins the other two, is glued along the front edge of the wrestplank. The nut is of stained beech and of a flat cross-section, tapering towards the player. It enters the case at both ends. Marks, probably of the original moderator retaining blocks, can be seen in the gap at the inside of the case on either side.

There is a large piece of sycamore running the length of the spine above the soundboard. This was probably added to strengthen the instrument and its place would probably once have been occupied by a simple moulded strip. There is an iron brace between the bellyrail and the wrestplank which helps to take up the tension of the strings.

The pearwood pawls, with springs of brass wire, lean forward towards the hammer shank beaks. The beech hammer shanks are all modern replacements. The hammer heads are of lime covered with replacement leather. The bumper rail for the pawls is of spruce and can be adjusted in and out because it is mounted in an oak rail (the upper limit of the keys) by means of dovetailed blocks which can move in the rail. The kapsels are of brass. The hammer rest blocks are later replacements. The single continuous check, of spruce, is no longer in its original position. It is triangular in cross-section and the long side of the curve is concave. The balance rail is of oak and pine. The keys are front guided. The front rail of the keyframe is of oak, the side walls are of lime and the remaining parts are of spruce or pine. The key levers are of lime.

The action slides into the case. A sledge, consisting of a framework of laths of spruce or pine, is then inserted under the action to raise it to the correct height under the strings. It is finished on the front surface with a piece of sycamore which forms the strip of wood visible below the keyboard.

The damper rest blocks curve up and away from each key to form platforms for each damper jack between each pair of keys. The dampers consist of damper jacks which move at their upper end through mortices in the ebonised damper house (of walnut ?) and at their lower ends through loops of (later) leather, attached to small sticks which are let into the damper house. Damper blocks are attached to the jacks. The bichord choirs have wedge-shaped dampers attached to the blocks and covered with leather, while the trichord choirs have leather applied straight onto the blocks.

Michael Latcham, who has examined this instrument in detail, concludes that many of its features are similar to features found on Viennese pianos by Anton Walter (1752–1826). These include the shape of the original moderator retaining blocks, the cross-sections of the bridge and to a lesser extent the nut, the iron gap-spacer, the way in which the pawl bumper rail can be adjusted, the cross-section of the check, the damper stools and the two soundboard ribs just visible in the treble. Other features, however, are most unlike those of Walter's pianos. These include the bass end of the bridge being jointed to the rest of the bridge, the arrangement of the legs and the skirting around the bottom of the case, the sledge under the action, the construction of the damper house and the three octave span. The influence of Walter is evident but the instrument is not by Walter himself. Other builders, such as Michael Rosenberger of Vienna and Johann Grober of Innsbruck, were also influenced by Walter, but the complete set of characteristics of this instrument points to no particular maker. It is most likely that the instrument is Austrian but provincial.

Most Austrian pianos of around the turn of the eighteenth century are not dated. Although the keyboard compass of such pianos is not an accurate means of dating them, the range $FF - c^4$ does not appear to have come into fashion until 1800 and seems to have rapidly been extended to six octaves. For this reason, Michael Latcham argues, a date of $c.1805$ would be a reasonable estimate, if this were a Viennese instrument. As it was probably not made in the capital, however, it could be a little later, making $c.1810$ plus or minus five years a good estimate. The ebony naturals and bone-capped sharps give no indication of date. Reversed keyboards were usually used in Austrian and south German pianos which were not mahogany-veneered until about 1810.

Michael Latcham

HISTORY OF THE INSTRUMENT

Provenance   Count Franz von Oppersdorff, Oberglogau
Paul de Wit, Leipzig, –1922
Rushworth and Dreaper Ltd, Liverpool, 1922–1967

A note in the Rushworth and Dreaper archives states that this instrument originally belonged to 'Count von Oppersdorff at Oberglogau Castle' and that it was played by his friend, Beethoven.

Count Franz von Oppersdorff (1778–1818) had his own orchestra at his castle of Oberglogau in Upper Silesia. He corresponded with Beethoven in 1808, after meeting him in 1806 during a visit to Prince Lichnowsky at Gratz. The two men became friends and the composer even dedicated his fourth symphony, Op.60, to the Count.

Rushworth and Dreaper purchased the instrument from Paul de Wit on 12th September, 1922, at a cost of '£4, plus expenses and duty, say £4, total cost £8.0.0'

REFERENCES

R & D catalogue 1 (undated), not paginated.
R & D catalogue 2 (undated), p.5.
Liverpool Echo, March 18, 1927, p.15.
The Liverpolitan, 1937, p.15.
James, 1970, p.141. pl.LXI.
Whittington-Egan, 1976, pp.158–159.
Bevan, 1990, p.68.

1.9. GRAND PIANO, John Broadwood and Sons, London, c.1840

Museum Accession Number 1972.162

TECHNICAL SPECIFICATION

Serial Number	14811
Nameboard Inscription	*Patent* *John Broadwood & Sons* *Manufacturers to Her Majesty* *Great Pulteney Street / Golden Square* *London*
Compass	6 Octaves and a fourth, CC – f^4
3-Octave-Span	498mm. Ivory naturals, ebony sharps
Stringing	Bichord throughout. Continuous hitch-plate with bolted frame.

	CC	c^2	f^4
Scaling	1570mm	301mm	56mm
Strike-Point	188mm	30mm	6.5mm
Gauges Extant	2.92mm (spun)	0.91mm	0.81mm

Action	English Grand. Overdampers to b^2
Stops	2 pedals: Piano by keyboard shift Damper lift
Case Size	Length 2280mm, Width 1240mm, Depth 310mm
Maker	John Broadwood and Sons (1808–)

DESCRIPTION

The case is veneered all over with mahogany and stands on three baluster-turned legs carved of solid mahogany, on brass castors. Both the tops of the legs, along the bottom section of the case, and the sweeping, outer sides of the keyboard, are decorated with carved, scrolling wing-shaped designs. The carving is missing from the leg at the tail end of the case and that on the front left leg is damaged. The wooden pedals and lyre-shaped pedal-stand are all of mahogany.

The inside lip of the case is also veneered with mahogany. The lid is of solid mahogany and is attached along the spine by three brass hinges. It has a hinged, folding front section and is strengthened along the underside by a batten of mahogany. It is supported by a small mahogany lid-prop, attached to the inside of the case on the right-hand side, and is secured by two internal brass clips on the bentside of the case, controlled by two carved knobs on the outside. The keyboard cover of solid mahogany folds back up into the keywell. The keyboard surround, keycheeks, and keyblocks are all veneered with rosewood. The nameboard is decorated at each side of the nameplate with an inlaid brass design of stylised foliage. The music stand and candle slides are all of solid mahogany. The keyfronts are of moulded boxwood.

The soundboard appears to be of spruce. The wrestplank and the yoke above the keyboard are both veneered with sycamore. The divided bridge and the nut are of beech. The strings are attached to a continuous cast iron hitch-plate, which has been screwed down over a narrower beech hitch-rail which can be seen running underneath.

Four large cast-iron bars and one smaller one are bolted to the wrestplank and run the length of the case, over the strings and onto the hitch-plate. The strings are held on the wrestplank by 156 iron wrest pins, which appear to be original. The serial number *14811* is stamped on the left-hand side of the wrestplank.

HISTORY OF THE INSTRUMENT

Provenance William Brougham, London, 1840–
Presented by Mr D.W.L. Burnham, 1972

A note in the Broadwood Archive states that this instrument was sent on hire to 'William Brougham Esqr, 19 Grosvenor Square', on 30th January, 1840. William Brougham (1795–1886) was M.P. for Southwark, 1831–1835, and a Master in Chancery, 1835–1840. In 1868 he succeeded to the title of second Baron Brougham and Vaux, on the death of his brother, Henry Peter Brougham, the first Baron.

1.10. SQUARE PIANO, Robertson and Co., London, c.1840–1845

Museum Accession Number 1966.370

Technical Specification

Serial Number	1595
Nameboard Inscription	*Robertson & Co* *Manufacturers of Improved Pianofortes, London*
Compass	6 Octaves and a fifth, CC – g^4
3-Octave-Span	493mm. Ivory naturals, ebony sharps
Stringing	17 singles – E, bichord – g^4 Iron hitch plate

	CC	c^2	g^4
Scaling	1543mm	282mm	45mm
Strike-Point	140mm	39mm	4mm
Gauges Extant	2.5mm (spun)	0.86mm	0.79mm

Action	English Double. No check
Stops	1 pedal: Damper lift
Case Size	Length 1865mm, Width 778mm, Depth 322mm

DESCRIPTION

The long rectangular case is veneered all over with mahogany. The lid, with hinged and folding front section and hinged keyboard flap, is also veneered with mahogany and crossbanded with it around the outer edge. One of the pedals is present but all the legs are now missing.

The keyboard surround, keycheeks and keyblocks are all veneered with mahogany. Above the keyboard, at either side, there are two areas of pierced, scrolling decoration, backed with red silk which has now shattered. The folding, adjustable music stand and the panels of scrolling fretwork at either side of it are all veneered with mahogany. The veneer on the panel on the left-hand side is splitting and lifting.

The soundboard appears to be of spruce, with a continuous cast-iron hitch-plate running along the right-hand side and back of the case.

This instrument is in very poor condition.

History of the Instrument

Provenance — Presented by Mrs Crisp, 1966

1.11. UPRIGHT PIANO, John Broadwood and Sons, London, 1853

Museum Accession Number 1983.3153.15

TECHNICAL SPECIFICATION

Serial Number	12250
Nameboard Inscription	*John Broadwood & Sons* *Manufacturers to Her Majesty* *Great Pulteney Street / Golden Square* *London*
Compass	6 Octaves and a sixth, CC – a^4
3-Octave-Span	491mm. Ivory naturals, ebony sharps
Stringing	6 singles – FF, bichord – a^4 Straight strung. Wooden frame

	CC	c^2	a^4
Scaling	946mm	290mm	42mm
Strike-Point	125mm	31mm	5mm
Gauges Extant	4.8mm (spun)	0.86mm	0.81mm

Action	Sticker, no check. Dampers to $c\#^3$
Stops	2 pedals: Piano by keyboard shift Damper lift
Case Size	Height 1210mm, Width 1292mm, Depth 680mm
Maker	John Broadwood and Sons (1808–)

DESCRIPTION

The case is veneered all over with zebrawood. The rectangular central panel, with beaded edge, in the upper part of the case is painted with a Classical scene of five women and a man in ancient Greek dress, grouped around a chariot and two horses, and flanked by three female goddesses (?), all on a gold ground and in a style similar to that of the sculptor John Flaxman. At the back of this panel is inscribed *Mr Snell Silk to Pattern fluted 12250* in pencil, indicating that it is a later replacement and that originally the rectangular space was filled with fluted silk fabric.

To each side of the central panel is a square panel of scrolling fretwork with a beaded edge, backed with red silk which is now shattered. The waist rail beading is now missing from one side of the case.

The underside of the keyboard fall has two solid square blocks of wood at either end, on which to stand candlesticks. The folding music stand is of mahogany. The keyboard surround, keycheeks and keyblocks are all ebonised, and the ebonised strip below the keyboard appears to be a later replacement, with six modern brass screws. The plain keyfronts are of boxwood. The keybed is signed *Sharp jn 21029*, probably a misprint for *12029*. It is fairly common for Broadwood actions to have a different serial number from the frame.

The lower section of the case is also decorated with a narrow band of scrolling fretwork across its width, backed with red silk which has now shattered. The two wooden panels are veneered with mahogany. The two free-standing front legs are turned at top and bottom, carved with scrolling acanthus leaf decoration at the 'knee', and of fluted, octagonal shape in the lower section, on brass castors.

The bottom lip of the case is stained all around, the result of water damage at some time during the past.

HISTORY OF THE INSTRUMENT

Provenance George Melly, Liverpool, 1853–
Presented by the Melly family, 1942

According to a record in the Broadwood Archive, Messrs Snell and Co., of Albermarle Street, London, supplied this instrument to Mr George Melly of Liverpool on 16th February, 1853. George Melly (1830–1894) was a member of a well-known Liverpool merchant family and Liberal M.P. for Stoke-on-Trent, 1868–1875.

This piano stood for many years in the Melly family's drawing room in their house at 90 Chatham Street, Liverpool.

1.12. UPRIGHT PIANO, Dreaper and Son, Liverpool, c.1860

Museum Accession Number 1967.161.15

TECHNICAL SPECIFICATION

Serial Numbers   4603, 1686, 3242

Nameboard Inscription   *By Their Majesties' Royal Letters Patent for England and France / Dreaper's / Compensating Bars and Harmonic Chambers / Agents in London and Paris / and at the Patentee's / 56 Bold Street Liverpool*

Compass   7 Octaves, AAA – a^4

3-Octave-Span   491mm. Ivory naturals, stained hardwood sharps

Stringing   Bichord throughout, straight-strung

	AAA	c^2	a^4
Scaling	1330mm	292mm	46mm
Strike-Point	133mm	27mm	4mm
Gauges Extant	3.3mm (spun)	0.95mm	0.75mm

Action   Sticker, no check. Dampers to a^2

Stops   2 pedals: Piano by hammer-rail shift / Damper lift

Case Size   Height 1787mm, Width 1346mm, Depth 705mm

Maker   William P. Dreaper and Son, later W.H. and G.H. Dreaper, (1828–1902)

DESCRIPTION   The case is of pine, veneered with quartered, crossbanded panels of tulipwood, and inlaid with broad bands of kingwood and boxwood stringing. The upper half of the case has three rectangular panels of fluted green silk, each one bordered with a decorative ormolu mount. The scrolling top of the case, and its edges, are also decorated with applied ormolu mounts in the Rococo style. The keyboard fall and the sides of the case are further decorated with five applied oval panels of flower-painted Sèvres porcelain, each one bordered with an ormolu mount.

In the lower half of the case, there are three square panels of quartered tulipwood veneer, each one bordered with kingwood veneer, boxwood stringing and an applied ormolu mount. The scrolling front legs, supported on the curving base of the case, are decorated with applied ormolu mounts in the form of female caryatids. The bottom lip of the case is veneered with tulipwood and decorated all around with an applied ormolu mount.

The keyboard surround, nameboard and keycheeks are veneered with rosewood and there is a folding music stand of solid tulipwood. The name is in the form of an applied transfer-print.

Andrew Garrett, adviser on musical instruments to the National Trust, has made a detailed examination of the instrument and has made the following observations. Despite its elaborate casework, the interior of the piano is relatively ordinary. The dampers, which extend up to a^2, are operated by tracker extensions from the stickers.

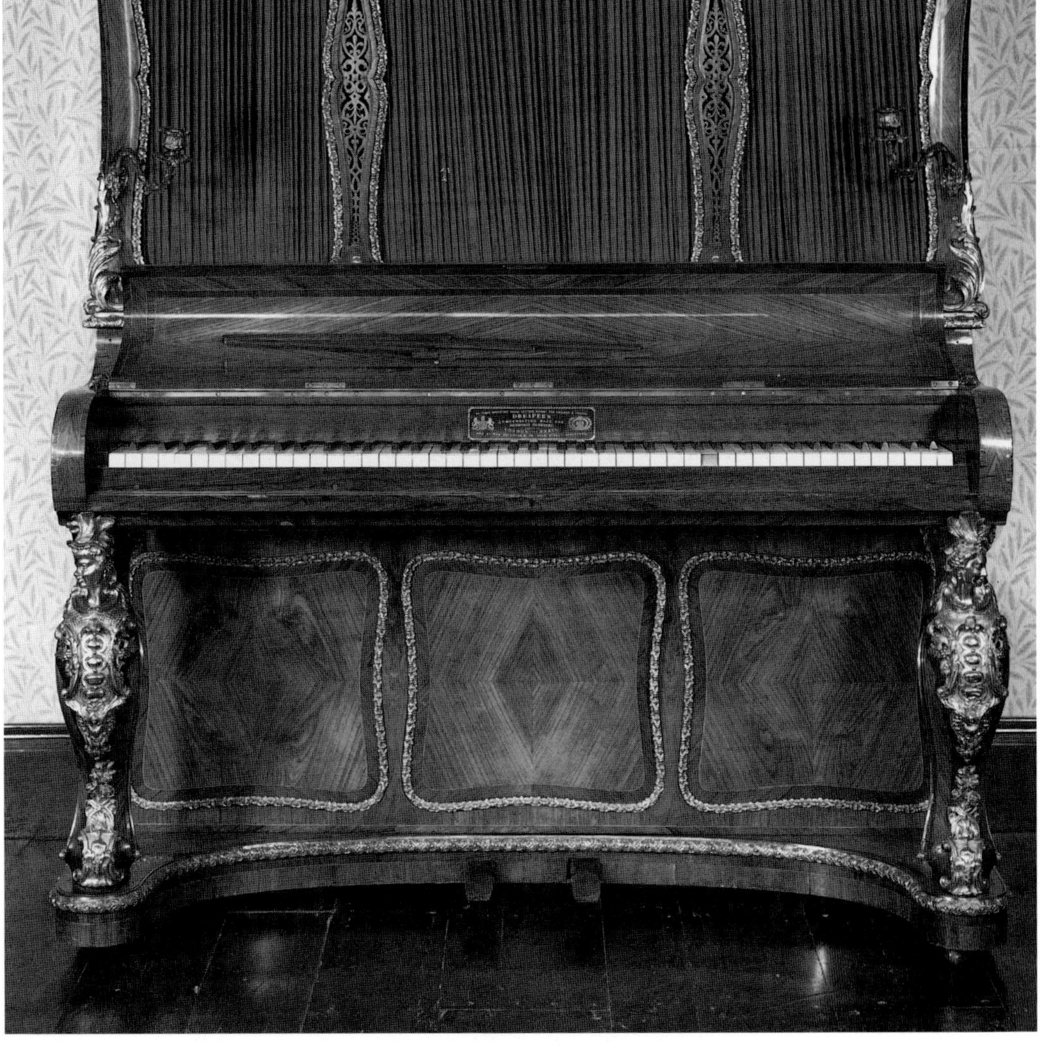

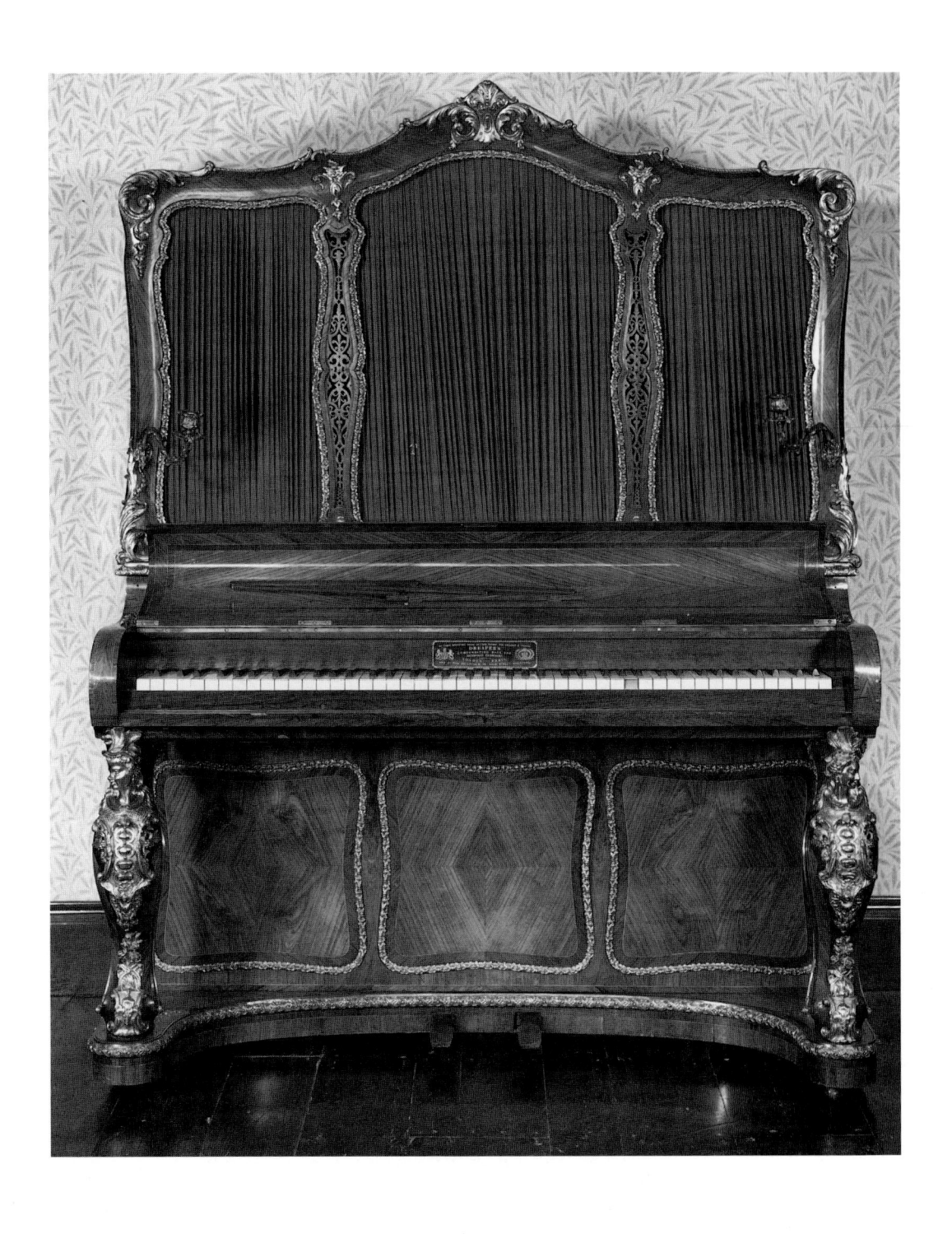

An iron plate provides individual hitching for each of the lowest 47 bichords (up to and including g^1), of which 23 are covered and pass over the bass bridge (AA – G). From GG# upwards, to prevent splitting of the sycamore rail, the strings pass around hitchpins which are arranged in clusters of three. Between c# and b^2, inadequate down-bearing at the nut has been remedied by the addition of 35 steel washers, secured by screws which are driven in between each close pair of strings.

The hoppers are mounted on bushed centres but the hinges throughout the rest of the action are of vellum. The strings and wrestpins are now badly rusted and the soundboard is split. The latter has also sunk, leaving the strings towards the bass end of the main bridge held down only by their draft pins. Where these have sheared, as at f#, the strings pass directly from nut pins to hitchpins and fail to touch the bridge at all. The shorter string of the g# bichord is broken.

Inscribed on the hammer rest rail are *Repaired, E. Pearson, Ap(ril ?) 1889* and *Keep Treble up, G.G. 1930*.

One unusual feature of this instrument is the inclusion at the back of the soundboard of 'compensating bars and harmonic chambers', as they were referred to by Dreaper's on the nameboard. Gradual sinking of the soundboard was more of a problem in pianos before the technique of 'doming' the board was adopted and a number of systems were devised by various manufacturers to prevent this happening while still retaining the necessary flexibility. Dreaper's scheme, patented on 19th December, 1854 (Patent No.2671), was for mounting between convenient frame members of the instrument as many additional struts, or 'compensating bars', as there were conventional soundbars. The struts were to effect a variable pressure on the soundbars by means of screw-mounted blocks, referred to as 'sound posts' in the Patent, and coil springs. In the tenor and bass of the compass, it was proposed that the struts should be hollow in section to act as 'generators of sound'. These were the so-called 'harmonic chambers', although they are not referred to as such in the Patent itself.

The remains of these 'compensating bars', with a number of their original screw-mounted blocks, can be seen on the underside of the soundboard, in the treble end.

On 21st May, 1861, Dreaper's took out another Patent (No.1293), with the intention of 'causing the tone or sound board to become convex on the side to which the strings are attached'. By this scheme, the curvature of the bars was to be achieved by means of 'metal tie-rods', passing through angle brackets mounted at the ends of each. Nuts and spring washers on the threaded ends of the rods applied the tension necessary to pull the bars into the arcuate form desired. The brackets were referred to as 'tone generators' in the Patent, although they were of no obvious accoustic benefit, and a shorter form of 'compensating bar' was included in the specification, possibly to prevent the soundboard from collapsing under the weight of the additional iron work.

Andrew Garrett

HISTORY OF THE INSTRUMENT

Provenance   Richard Watt, Liverpool
Rushworth and Dreaper Ltd, Liverpool, 1928–1967

This piano was made to order by Dreaper's for Richard Watt (1835–1865) of Speke Hall, Liverpool, for the Blue Drawing Room there. It was made to match a suite of furniture, upholstered in pale blue silk, in the French Rococo style.

A note in Rushworth and Dreaper's archives states that they bought it back 'from Speke Hall' in 1928 at a cost of £10.

Today, Speke Hall is owned and run by the National Trust. The piano is on long loan to the Trust and can be seen once again in its original setting in the Blue Drawing Room.

REFERENCES   Taylor, 1976, front cover.
Whittington-Egan, 1976, p.158.

1.13. UPRIGHT PIANO, H. Justin Browne, London, c.1870

Museum Accession Number 1985.582

TECHNICAL SPECIFICATION

Serial Number	2382
Nameboard Inscription	*By Her Majesty's Royal Letters Patent* *Irresistible Piano Forte* *Manufactured expressly for extreme climates* *H. Justin Browne* *237, 239, Euston Road / London / Tottenham Court Rd*
Retailer's Inscription	*Crane & Sons Ltd* *Liverpool & London*
Compass	7 Octaves, AAA – a^4
3-Octave-Span	491mm. Ivory naturals, ebony sharps
Stringing	8 singles – EE, bichord – b^2, trichord – a^5 Straight strung. Wooden frame

	AAA	c^2	a^4
Scaling	1061mm	302mm	49mm
Strike-Point	165mm	40mm	8mm
Gauges Extant	5.46mm (spun)	0.94mm	0.81mm
Gauge Marks	–	16	13

Action	Sticker, no check. Dampers to a^2
Stops	2 pedals: Piano by hammer-rail shift 　　　　　Damper lift
Case Size	Height 1260mm, Width 1325mm, Depth 628mm
Maker	H. Justin Browne (1864–1909)
Retailer	Crane and Sons (1850–) Continues as Bell and Crane Music Ltd

DESCRIPTION

The case is of pine, veneered all over with walnut. The central panel in the upper part of the case is decorated with a transfer-printed design of scrolling flowers and leaves, in imitation of marquetry inlay, with a carved and applied acanthus-leaf scroll at either side. Both candlesticks are now missing from the panel but the screw-holes for their mounts are still visible. Originally, the space now occupied by the panel was probably filled by fluted silk or fretwork panels and it is probably a later replacement.

　The maker's name, in the form of a transfer-print, is applied to the underside of the keyboard fall. The present folding mahogany music stand is a later replacement and the screw-holes for the original are visible. The keyboard surround, keycheeks and keyblocks are all veneered with walnut.

　The lower part of the case is also veneered with walnut, in two long rectangular fielded panels. The front legs are in the form of scrolling S-shapes, boldly carved with acanthus leaf decoration, and supported on two curving blocks running from the bottom of the case. The wooden pedals are veneered with mahogany.

There is a matching piano stool, with upholstered swivel seat and scrolling acanthus-leaf carved legs.

HISTORY OF THE INSTRUMENT

Provenance   Presented by Mrs I.M. Marriott, 1985

The history of this piano, when new, is not known but it was sold second-hand by Crane's to the donor's parents in 1920, for £21.0.0. It is typical of the thousands of pianos sold by Crane's, who specialised in the sale of their own and other manufacturers' pianos, organs and harmoniums.

The firm was founded in Liverpool in 1850 and its early premises were in Cooper's Buildings, Church Street. By the 1890s, they also had a large factory in Scotland Road where they manufactured their own instruments. They became a Limited Company in 1897, and the business expanded so that by the early years of the twentieth century there were Cranes branches in many major cities, including London, Manchester, Birmingham, Sheffield, Cardiff, Glasgow, Belfast and Dublin.

In 1913 their main premises moved to Hanover Street, Liverpool, to the site it still occupies today. During the early 1980s the firm was taken over by the German instrument manufacturer, Hohner. They continue to trade today under the name of Bell and Crane Music Limited.

1.14. UPRIGHT PIANO, designed by W. and G. Audsley, made by W.H. and G.H. Dreaper, Liverpool, *c.*1878

Museum Accession Number 1988.355

TECHNICAL SPECIFICATION

Serial Numbers	3990, 2591
Nameboard Inscription	*96 Bold Street* *Wm.H. & G.H. Dreaper* *Late Wm.P. Dreaper & Son* *Liverpool*
Keyblock Label	*W & G Audsley* *Architects* *Liverpool*
Compass	7 Octaves and a third, AAA – c^5
3-Octave-Span	498mm. Ivory naturals, ebony sharps
Stringing	12 singles – GG, 15 bichord – B, trichord – c^5 Obliquely straight-strung. Half frame

	AAA	c^2	c^5
Scaling	1176mm	320mm	47mm
Strike-Point	150mm	34mm	0mm
Gauges Extant	5.4mm (spun)	0.89mm	0.81mm

Action	Tape-check. Dampers to $c\#^3$
Stops	2 pedals: Piano by moderator/celeste Damper lift
Case Size	Height 1320mm, Width 1462mm, Depth 628mm
Makers	W.H. and G.H. Dreaper (1828–1902)
Designers	William James and George Ashdown Audsley, active *c.*1857–1883
DESCRIPTION	The case is completely ebonised. The central panel in the upper part of the case is divided into three sections, a rectangular panel flanked by two square ones. All three panels are composed of fretwork in the form of stylised lotus flowers, highlighted with gold paint and bordered with a Greek key pattern, backed with modern gold-coloured fabric. The outer edges of the two square panels are each decorated with two tapering pilasters, with lotus flower-shaped capitals, highlighted with gold paint, beneath a reeded rim and decorative border. The squared keyboard fall is decorated around the front edge with incised gold lotus flowers, the design continuing in a band around the sides of the case, above a reeded rim. The keyboard surround, keycheeks and keyblocks are all ebonised and at each side of the keyboard there is a carved sphinx. The maker's name is inlaid into the underside of the lid in brass letters, surrounded by a brass border, and flanked on either side by a bronze medal. The medal on the left bears a Classical female head in profile and *Republique Francaise*. That on the right is inscribed *Exposition Universelle Internationale de 1878 Paris*. The designers' names

are inscribed on a small brass plaque inlaid in the right-hand keyblock.

The lower half of the case is divided into three plainly ebonised panels, flanked at the outer edges of the case by a fluted pilaster with lotus flower-shaped capital, highlighted with gold paint. The two front legs, supported on block bases extending at right angles from the bottom of the case, are also in the form of fluted columns with lotus flower-shaped capitals, all highlighted with gold paint.

HISTORY OF THE INSTRUMENT

Provenance Dan Klein Ltd, London
Purchased at auction, Sotheby's, 17th June, 1988, lot number 271

It is not known if this instrument was made by Dreaper's for a particular customer or simply as a showpiece for exhibition. It was owned by the dealer, Dan Klein Ltd, of Halkin Arcade, Belgravia, London, before being purchased from Sotheby's by the Museum in 1988.

Dreaper's commissioned William James and George Ashdown Audsley, a well-known firm of Liverpool architects, to produce the design. William Audsley began in business around 1857, and was based in Upper Stanhope Street, Liverpool. Between 1865 and 1875 the brothers were in business in Harrington Street, but by the time this piano was commissioned they had moved to the Law Association Buildings in Cook Street, Liverpool.

Like Owen Jones, the Audsleys produced several books on pattern and design, including *Polychromatic Decoration* (1882) and *The Practical Decorator and Ornamentist* (1892).

REFERENCES

Exhibition catalogue, Paris Universal International Exhibition, 1878, p.64.
Conner (ed.), 1983, p.103, no.215.
Sale catalogue, Sotheby's, 17th June, 1988, p.68, lot 271.

1.15. UPRIGHT PIANO, George Rogers and Sons, London, *c*.1909

Museum Accession Number 1974.261

TECHNICAL SPECIFICATION

Serial Numbers	Case 24036, Action 23954, Frame R & S 208
Nameboard Inscription	*George Rogers & Sons* *London*
Retailer's Inscription	*Argyle Street / Ryalls & Jones Ltd / Birkenhead*
Compass	7 Octaves, AAA – a^4
3-Octave-Span	492mm. Synthetic ivory naturals, ebony sharps
Stringing	10 singles – FF#, 22 bichord – e, trichord – a^4 Straight strung. Iron frame

	AAA	c^2	a^4
Scaling	867mm	335mm	58mm
Strike-Point	107mm	39mm	2mm
Gauges Extant	6mm (Double spun)	0.94mm	0.81mm
Gauges Marked	–	16 ½	14

Action	Tape-check. Underdampers – f^3
Stops	2 pedals: Piano by half-blow Damper lift
Case Size	Height 1125mm, Width 1365mm, Depth 612mm
Maker	George Rogers and Sons (1843–1983)
Retailer	Ryalls and Jones (1890–1948)

DESCRIPTION	The plain case is veneered all over with rosewood. The central panel in the upper half of the case is crossbanded with tulipwood and inlaid with two lines of a darker wood stringing. There are two brass candlesticks, cast in a flowing Art Nouveau style, attached to the front panel.
	    The keyboard surround, keycheeks and keyblocks are all ebonised. The maker's name is transfer-printed in gold letters on the underside of the keyboard fall, and the retailer's name is transfer-printed onto the keyboard surround. The folding music stand is veneered with rosewood and fits into the top of the case.
	    The front supports are grooved and curve out from beneath the keyboard, resting on blocks which run out at right angles from the bottom of the case. The pedals are of brass.

HISTORY OF THE INSTRUMENT

Provenance	Presented by Mr K.P. Lewis, 1974

1.16. OCTAVE SPINET, Chickering and Sons, Boston, USA, 1910

Museum Accession Number 1967.161.16

TECHNICAL SPECIFICATION

Serial Number	65
Soundboard Inscription	Made-by-Chickering-&-Sons Boston USA
	under-the-direction-of MCMX
	Arnold-Dolmetsch- No 65
Compass	4 Octaves, $c - c^4$
3-Octave-Span	476mm. Fruitwood naturals, walnut sharps
Stringing	1 x 4 foot

	c	c^3	c^4
Scaling	744mm	161mm	81mm
Pluck-Point	58mm	52mm	44mm
Gauges Extant	0.52mm	0.23mm	0.23mm

Action	Single manual. Single register of jacks
Case Size	Length 828mm, Width 516mm, Depth 132mm
Makers	Chickering and Sons (1823–1932)
	Arnold Dolmetsch (1858–1940)

DESCRIPTION

The irregular trapezium-shaped case is of pine, painted white, with painted gilt 'stringing' along the sides and along the underside and edges of the lid. The lid is attached to the back of the case by three shaped brass hinges. It has a folding front section, hinged along its length with another three shaped brass hinges, and a hinged keyboard flap. The music stand is formed by the keyboard flap itself and by an applied lip attached to the underside of the folding section of the lid.

The inner lip of the case, sitting on top of the soundboard, the keyboard surround, the carved keycheeks and the keyblocks are all of pencil cedar, as are the jackrail and the small lid-prop fitted to the inner right side of the case. The keys have arcaded fronts.

The soundboard appears to be of spruce. The nut and bridge are both of beech. The hitchpin rail, running along the inner right-hand side of the case, is of cedar. The strings are held by 48 steel wrest pins, which appear to be original, on the wrestplank, which is veneered with sycamore.

The maker's name is painted on the left-hand side of the soundboard.

HISTORY OF THE INSTRUMENT

Provenance

Mr Alcock, Liverpool, –1938
Rushworth and Dreaper Ltd, Liverpool, 1938–1967

A note in the archives of Rushworth and Dreaper states that they bought this instrument in April 1938 from a Mr Alcock, of the Midland Bank, Commutation Row, Liverpool, for the sum of £3.10.0.

Arnold Dolmetsch, a French-born musician and instrument maker, and his family, were largely responsible for the late nineteenth-century revival of interest in early music. Dolmetsch specialised in the reproduction of early keyboard, string and wind instruments. Between 1905 and 1910 he worked for Chickering and Sons, supervising the making of harpsichords, clavichords, spinets, lutes and other stringed instruments.

Spinet, Gaveau, Paris, 1926

Organs

2.1. POSITIVE ORGAN, Nicolaus Manderscheid, Nuremberg, 1644

Museum Accession Number 1967.161.5

TECHNICAL SPECIFICATION

Internal Label

Nicolaus Manderscheid
Orgellmacher
Dsn
Nurmbergh
1644

3-Octave-Span 487mm. Burr sycamore-capped naturals, rosewood-capped sharps

Compass 4 Octaves, C – c³, short octave, omitting C#, D#, F# and G#

Action Tracker

Stops Bass: Fagot (8 foot)
Principal (1½ foot Quint)
Waldflote (2 foot)
Klein Gedacht (4 foot)
Gr(osse ?) Gedacht (8 foot)
Treble: Principal (1½ foot Quint)

Case Size Height 880mm, Width 920mm, Depth 675mm

Stand Size Height 745mm, Width 975mm, Depth 710mm

Maker Nicolaus Manderscheid (1580–1662)

DESCRIPTION

The organ is housed in a plain-fronted oak case, with two doors, which has been painted a brown-green colour. Both doors sit on iron, 'spike' hinges, from which they can be easily removed for ease of access. At each side of the case there are two square iron brackets, for housing the carrying bars, and a removable, wooden 'grilled' panel for interior inspection and access.

The plain oak stand has four slightly angled legs of almost square proportion. They are strengthened by stretchers between the front and back legs, and a horizontal stretcher between both of these. There are two carrying poles of oak, each padded at the ends with straw-filled blue linen fabric. All four ends have been covered with natural-coloured linen to protect the original during display (1993).

With the organ doors open, the 45 metal pipes of the Principal rank can be seen, arranged so that the pipe-mouths run parallel to the intricately-designed and pierced toe-board of 'hump-back' design. The smallest pipes occupy the highest point of the toe board. The elaborately carved and gilded pipe shades are in the form of a central Grotesque face, with billowing acanthus leaves issuing from its mouth to either side, and similar corner sections.

The naturals of the keyboard are made of oak, capped with a burr sycamore, and the sharps are of oak capped with rosewood. The carved keyfronts are of ogee design. The sides of the 'head' of each key are chamfered at an angle of 30 degrees. There are 45 keys but 46 channels, the result of the splitting of the key D#/E flat. This was a common seventeenth century practice.

The keyboard cheeks are square wooden compartments, housing the metal levers that operate the mechanism for stop selection. There are five levers in allotted rectangular spaces on the left-hand side of the keyboard and one lever on the right-hand side. The names of all the stops are written on paper labels, positioned to the right of the levers which activate the stops.

There are 225 pipes; the 45 Principal pipes are of metal alloy (25 of these are original and the other 20 are later replacements), the 45 Fagot pipes, of square section, are of lead, and the remaining 135 are of wood.

There are two folding leather bellows, which are attached to the top of the organ case at the right-hand side. They are activated by two hinged wooden poles on the left-hand side of the organ. These would have been operated by the player's assistant or assistants. The bellows have been restored in the fairly recent past, probably by Rushworth and Dreaper during the 1960s, and new seals have been attached to their folds. Some of the original lining paper, composed of old manuscript pages, can still be seen on the folds.

The wind trunk is made from pine and leads from the treble end of the bellows to the wind-chest. The wind-chest is made from oak, and has an oak face-board, covered in leather and held in place by iron brackets.

The keys are connected to the wind-chest by means of stickers, which cause the pallet to open when a key is depressed.

Alan Barnes

HISTORY OF THE INSTRUMENT

Provenance

Paul de Wit, Leipzig, 1923
Rushworth and Dreaper Ltd, Liverpool, 1923–1967

For almost 300 years, this organ stood in the Gangolfskirche in Bamberg, Bavaria. It was used to accompany choral singing in the church, and for processional services such as the annual Feast of Corpus Christi, when it was carried through the streets of Bamberg, on its two carrying-poles, by four bearers. It is believed to be the oldest extant positive organ by Manderscheid still in its original state. An earlier example by the same maker, dating from the 1620s, is located in the Pankratiuskapelle in Bamberg but is in a much altered state.

Records relating to the Gangolf instrument, from the Church Committee Sessions and the Church Annual Accounts, can be found in the Bamberg State Archives. The Annual Accounts include an entry, dated 30th November 1652, for two measures of pear wine, as part payment for repairs to the organ. Later entries detail expenses for the carriers, for the tuning of the organ and the making of new pipes. Other documents, dating from 1826 onwards, are located in the Gangolf Parish Archives. They include details of the repair of the organ in 1883 by the organ builder Karl Hansen, for the sum of 20 florins.

The organ became unplayable during the early 1890s, through damage to the bellows and the disappearance of some 20 pipes (believed to have been stolen by the Sacristan's assistant at Gangolf). It was put into store in a small room in the church, next to the Chapel of Divine Help, and it remained there until the summer of 1923 when it was re-discovered and purchased by the Dutch collector, Paul de Wit. He subsequently sold it to Rushworth and Dreaper on 13th November, 1923 for the sum of £65. With expenses (but no duty) of £8.7.10, Rushworths spent a total of £73.7.10 on its acquisition, and a further £17 on 'organ works' once it had reached Britain.

REFERENCES

R & D catalogue 1 (undated), not paginated.
R & D catalogue 2 (undated), p.6.
The Liverpolitan, 1937, p.14.
Spiegl, 1972, pp.42–43.
Taylor, 1976, p.101.
Schindler, undated, not paginated.
Bevan, 1990, pp.68–69.

2.2. CHAMBER ORGAN, John Snetzler, London, 1767

Museum Accession Number 1967.161.1

TECHNICAL SPECIFICATION

Case Inscription	*J. Snetsler, Londini Fecit, 1767*
3-Octave-Span	487mm. Ivory naturals, ebony sharps
Compass	4 Octaves and a third, C – e^3, 53 notes
Action	Tracker

Stops	Bass : Sesquialtra (2 ranks), bass – note b, metal
	    Flute (4 foot), wood
	    Stop Diapason (8 foot), metal
	Treble : Cornet (2 ranks), treble, metal
	    Fifteenth (2 foot) wood/metal
	    Open Diapason, wood

Case Size	Height 2690mm, Width 1140mm, Depth 870mm
Maker	John Snetzler (1710–1785)

DESCRIPTION

The case is made from oak, veneered and crossbanded with mahogany and sycamore and inlaid with a lighter wood stringing. The front of the case is divided into three sections, each housing non-speaking, flat-backed display pipes. There are six gilt wooden pipes in the two outer, side compartments and 11 in the central compartment. The feet of the display pipes sit on a curved toe-board of 'hump-backed' design. The toe-board is veneered with mahogany and inlaid with a dark and a light wood stringing. The tops of the display pipes are shaded by a pierced and gilt inverted triangular carving in the form of scrolling acanthus leaves.

The top of the case is surmounted by a broken pediment. The name inscription, painted in gold capital letters, appears on the narrow frieze immediately below the pediment. The name is protected by glass and framed in mahogany. This was not Snetzler's usual method of signing his work. His signature, on a piece of paper, was normally attached to the back of the wind-chest, and the 'signature' on this instrument was probably painted on at some later date, possibly during the nineteenth century.

The case originally had folding and hinged doors, of either solid wood or glass in a wooden framing. The original hinge mortices and bolt-holes have now been filled in with wooden blocks.

The lower section of the case, below the keyboard, consists of a cupboard for the bellows and the reservoir. It has two doors of oak veneered with mahogany, each held in place by hinges placed on the outside edge. Their elliptical-shaped centres are crossbanded with mahogany and inlaid at the edges with a lighter wood stringing.

There are three narrow slots cut into the bottom of the doors, one in the centre and one each to left and right. The slots originally accommodated the iron foot pedals. The left-hand pedal was for a 'shifting' or 'machine' movement device, used for reducing full organ to foundation tone. It controlled additional, separate sliders mounted in the wind-chest, immediately above the individual stop-sliders, and operated by wooden trundles and iron rods. This mechanism has now been removed. The right pedal supplied wind to the feeder and the wedge reservoir, and the central pedal controlled the swell mechanism.

The two sides of the case are identical, each consisting of solid mahogany panels, a large rectangular one in the upper section and a smaller, square one in the lower section.

The present keyboard, although old, is not the original. An original Snetzler keyboard would have had incised horizontal lines running across the playing surface of the keys, and the naturals would probably have been of ebony, rather than ivory, with chamfered sides to the heads. The ivory naturals of the present keyboard have moulded boxwood fronts.

The keyboard surround, both above and below, is veneered with mahogany, crossbanded with sycamore and inlaid with a light wood stringing. The carved keyboard blocks are of solid mahogany. The six stop-knobs at the sides of the keyboard are of turned ivory. They have been labelled with rectangular bone labels, glued at the side of each stop. Each stop-knob is inserted into a square mahogany shank, connected to an internal shank of oak or deal, and then to the soundboard slider.

The pin-action soundboard is made from solid oak and was restored by Rushworth and Dreaper during the late 1970s. The front face-board is also of oak, and the rectangular rackboard is a replacement, although the original is retained in the Museum.

There are 287 pipes, 103 of tin, 80 of lead and 104 of wood. They are all original, except for the two ranks of Sesquialtra pipes and the two ranks of Cornet pipes, of English tin and pure lead, which are all replacements by Rushworth and Dreaper of the late 1970s.

The remains of the original swell action, in the form of a hinged lid or trap door, can be seen in the roof of the organ. There is a pulley located just below the swell lid for guiding the rope which would have been attached to it, linking it with the swell foot pedal via a wooden roller connected to a vertical pole.

The original wind system, consisting of a feeder and wedge reservoir, is still present. The bellows were re-leathered during the late 1970s by Rushworth and Dreaper. They are operated by a foot pedal located at the right-hand side of the case. This pedal would have been pumped by an assistant and was possibly re-located in this position in 1978, when the organ was last played. Originally, the foot pedal for the bellows would have been located at the front of the case on the right-hand side.

Alan Barnes

History of the instrument

Provenance Rushworth and Dreaper Ltd, Liverpool, 1925–1967

The original owner of this instrument is unknown. According to records in the archives of Rushworth and Dreaper, they purchased it 'at auction from Gilbert, Ashley House, Frodsham', in April 1925. It cost £10 and a further £10 was spent on it for 'organ works' thereafter.

It is unclear, from the above reference, exactly who 'Gilbert' was but this could refer to a dealer or auctioneer. Ashley House, in Main Street, Frodsham, near Chester, was built in the 1830s and was occupied by a Miss Ashley. During the 1920s it was bought by an Edward Greenway, who established a veterinary practice there, but it is not known if the organ was owned by him or by an earlier occupier of the house.

REFERENCES

R & D catalogue 1 (undated), not paginated.
R & D catalogue 2 (undated), p.7.
The Liverpolitan, 1937, p.14.
Wilson, 1968, p.108, no.16, fig.8.
Barnes, 1982, Vol.2, p.191.
Bevan, 1990, p.68.
Barnes and Renshaw, 1993, pp.148–149.

2.3. BOTTLE-ORGAN, Johann Samuel Kühlewein, Eisleben, 1798

Museum Accession Number 1967.161.14

TECHNICAL SPECIFICATION

Nameboard Inscription *Ich bin verfertigt von Johann Samuel Kühlewein in Eisleben in der Graf schaft Mansfeld im jahr 1798*

3-Octave-Span 481mm. Ebony naturals, bone-capped sharps

	Piano	**Organ**
Compass	5 Octaves and 2 notes, FF – g³	4 Octaves and a fifth, C-g³
Disposition		8-foot C-F Wooden stopped pipes F# – g³ Bottles 4-foot C-g³ Bottles
Stringing	Bichord throughout	

	FF	c²	g³
Scaling	1633mm	332mm	94mm
Strike-Point	117mm	20mm	18.5mm
Gauges Marked	–	3	5

Action	Viennese with escapement and backcheck	Pin action
Stops	4 Pedals Piano on/off Moderator Dampers Organ pump – also handle behind	4 Handstops 8 foot on/off 4 foot on/off Organ on/off C-b Organ on/off c¹-g³

Case Size Length 1843mm, Width 698mm, Height 2230mm

DESCRIPTION

Square pianos with organs attached are not uncommon and usually look like pianos with a slightly deeper case to accommodate the pipes of the organ. Such instruments are often described as 'organised pianos'. This example, however, has glass bottles instead of pipes and has therefore generally been referred to as a bottle-organ.

According to information in Rushworth and Dreaper's archives, this instrument was made for an unnamed church situated on the island of Heligoland, off the coast of Germany, which was difficult to reach from the mainland. It was believed that, due to the remote location of the church, glass bottles filled with inert wax were used in the organ, rather than pipes which would have been more susceptible to changes in climatic conditions and would probably have required re-tuning by an organ-builder from the mainland. This explanation of the instrument's origin has not, so far, been substantiated and it is possible that the bottles were used simply to produce a purer tone, as with the glass harmonica of around the same period.

The main body of the case is of pine veneered with mahogany. Originally it was much plainer, and the three ebonised, applied diamond shapes on the front of the case are later additions. The two tambour doors at the front of the case, which conceal the two ranks of bottles and which slide up to open, and the two dummy tambour doors at either side of the case, are later additions. Originally, the door apertures at the front may have been filled with silk screens, or even swell shutters, and the sides of the case may have been plain, without any openings at all. The moulding around all four doors is also of a later date.

The open frieze along the top of the hood is probably contemporary with the ebonised diamonds on the case front, and with the fretwork panel on the right-hand side of the stand, which conceals the bellows. Some of the moulding on the hood may also be of a later date than the rest of the case. The lowest concave moulding on the hood and the convex moulding on the top of the case are each of different construction and are not outlined with ebony as are all other parts of the casework. The hood is signed *W. Parr 1948, 1952* and *W.J. Parr 3/6/64* on the inside.

The stand originally had only the four outside legs, which are made from oak veneered with mahogany. Kühlewein's original design of leg attachment was not completely satisfactory and subsequent modifications at various dates increased the already considerable weight of the instrument, resulting in weakening of the structure. To overcome this problem, two additional legs, made of oak and stained in imitation of mahogany, were added on the inside of the stand. Attempts to stabilise the legs in the past have included fitting battens to the end of the case and large iron straps to the rear of the corner joint. Neither of these remedies proved effective and, to give added support to the weak legs, wooden stretchers were fixed to them by steel angle-brackets. The pedal-stretcher is probably the only original one and this has been cut-down.

The pedals date from three different periods. The left pedal is of oak, veneered with mahogany, and appears to be original. The centre two appear to be later replacements of oak and are fitted to similar unusual hinges. The extreme right-hand bellows pedal, also of oak, appears to be the most recent and is fitted to a conventional hinge.

The piano is a typical German/Viennese instrument from the turn of the eighteenth century. The soundboard is probably made from spruce and the bridge from maple. The bridge has been broken and the soundboard torn along the grain, probably due to excessive tension of the strings. The strings are not original, dating either from around 1914 or from much later. Due to the damage they were causing they have now been removed from the soundboard altogether. The compass of the piano is five octaves and two notes, and the action is Viennese with escapement and hammer back-check. The hammers are leather-covered and are pivoted in brass kapsels. The over-dampers are spring-assisted with leather-covered wedges and flat pads. To turn the piano off, the first pedal operates a sliding rail that removes the escapement levers. The second pedal operates a moderator rail, and the third pedal is a damper-lift.

The piano is supported on the stand, which also houses the bellows, with a foot pedal and pump handle at the rear of the case. The wind is conveyed by a trunk to the pallet chest. It would appear that the present bellows were added some time before 1914, since Ehrenhofer's article of that year describes the previous poor wind supply from the 'single fold bellows' and the construction of a larger bellows and the decorative panels to hide them. A glue line can be seen along the lower edge of the case, indicating that there was probably a bottom on this section of the instrument with the original, smaller bellows inside it.

Handstops at each end of the keyboard operate removable

intermediate levers which are fitted under the keyboard. It is therefore possible to switch off the organ at either bass or treble end with division at middle c. These intermediate levers operate short stickers above the pin-operated pallets. These pallets are housed in a grooved board which conveys the wind to the rear of the instrument where the stop-change sliders are situated. Stop-change between 4 foot and 8 foot is effected by lockable levers underneath the keyboard.

Above the sliders is a vertical row of wooden wind-feed pipes to another grooved board that distributes the wind to the bottles. There are two ranks of bottles, one at 4 foot and one at 8 foot pitch, arranged in four rows alternately. Each bottle is attached to a wooden 'sledge' by means of two brass straps, with a leather strip protecting the bottle from the strap. The 106 bottles are all different sizes and must have been blown specially for the instrument. The two largest bottles are not original. Rough tuning has been achieved by partial filling of the bottles with red wax. Tuning or voicing of the bottles has been achieved by grinding the mouth apertures. Fine tuning and voicing was effected by manipulating and directing the lead feed-tube and the lead flap soldered to it. The 'flags' in front of the bottle-necks probably served the same purpose as beards in pipes. The 8 foot rank of pipes is supplemented by six wooden stopped pipes which are located under the wind-conveyance board. There is an indecipherable signature, dated 1913, on one of these pipes.

David Hunt

HISTORY OF THE INSTRUMENT

Provenance

Paul de Wit, Leipzig, –1922
Rushworth and Dreaper Ltd, Liverpool, 1922–1967

It is not known exactly how this instrument came to be in the collection of Paul de Wit, but a record in the archives of Rushworth and Dreaper states that they purchased it from him on 10th October, 1922, at a cost of £15 plus duty and expenses of about £9, which brought the total cost to £24. Rushworth's then carried out some 'organ works' on the instrument, which cost a further £12.

REFERENCES

R & D catalogue 1 (undated), not paginated.
R & D catalogue 2 (undated), p.7.
Ehrenhofer, 1914, pp.584–588.
The Liverpolitan, 1937, pp.14–15.
Spiegl, 1972, p.43.
Whittington-Egan, 1976, p.158.
Remnant, 1978, p.111.
Bevan, 1990, p.68.

2.4. CHURCH ORGAN CONSOLE, Robert Hope-Jones, Birkenhead, 1897

Museum Accession Number 1983.2091.1

TECHNICAL SPECIFICATION

Nameboard Inscription *The Hope-Jones Organ Company Limited*
Protected by Royal Letters Patent

Nameboard Label *Tuning and Regulation. This organ is in the care of Wm. Hill & Son and Norman & Beard Ltd, London*

3-Octave-Span 486mm. Synthetic ivory naturals, stained synthetic ivory sharps

Compass Upper manual, 5 Octaves, C – c⁴, 61 notes
Lower manual, 5 Octaves, C – c⁴, 61 notes
Pedals, C – f, 30 notes

Action Electric

Stops

Pedal Organ :
Tibia Profunda 16
(Tibia)
In Two Powers. Double 16 (from Great)
(Bourd)
Diaphonic Horn 16
(Diaph)
Great to Pedals 8
(Great)
Swell to Pedals 8
(Swell)

Great Organ :
Rohr Gedact 16
(Double)
Tibia Plena 8
(Tibia)
Open Diapason 8
(Open)
Hohl Flute 8
(Flute)
Viol D'Amour 8
(Viol)
Harmonic Flute 4
(Flute)
Super Octave 4
(Great)
Swell to Great sub 16
(Swell)
Double Touch (Swell to Great Unison 8)
(Swell)
Swell to Great Super 4
(Swell)

Swell Organ :
Lieblich Gedact 8
(Gedt)
Viol D'Orchestre 8
(Viol)
Echo Salicional 8
(Salc)
Vox Angelica 8
(Vox)
Gemshorn 4

        (Gems)
        Cornopean 8
        (Corno)
        Sub Octave 16
        (Swell)
        Super Octave 4
        (Swell)

Console Size   Height 1245mm, Width 1420mm, Depth 610mm

Maker   Robert Hope-Jones (1859–1914)

Description   This organ console, together with the electric switch relayboard, pedalboard and stop-slider motor box, is typical of the work of Robert Hope-Jones. The console is made from oak, with the words *Laus Deo* carved on each side. The roll-top keyboard cover and folding music stand are also of oak. The legs are arranged at right angles to the main body of the console.

           There are three composition pedals to the Great and Pedal organs (marked p.f.ff.) three composition pedals to the Swell organ (marked p.f.ff.) and a disconnected pedal to the right of the console, probably for duplicating the Stop-Switch Selector. There is also a balanced Swell pedal.

           The natural keys of both manuals are of synthetic ivory and the sharps are stained black, as are the keyboard cheeks. Above the upper manual, to the left, there is a voltmeter and in the centre a 'power on' light.

The stop switches or keys are of ivory and are positioned horizontally immediately below the music stand. They are pivoted on a single wire, which runs through their centres, and are grouped in departments. The names of the departments, together with colour-codings, are printed above the stop keys on a strip of ivory. The keys are coded white for flue-stops, red for reeds and green for couplers. The departmental and tonal classifications are shown on the stop keys themselves. A further, brown stop key, marked *Stop Switch*, is positioned to the left of the Swell stop key. This causes the electric circuit to be broken, enabling the organist to prepare registration in advance.

Insulated wires in small cables lead from the testboard to the other side of the soundboard. Here, electro-pneumatic levers open air valves beneath the pipes. A long flexible cable connects the console to the organ.

The organ's rectangular cast iron bellows-weight, marked *Hope-Jones*, also survives.

Alan Barnes

HISTORY OF THE INSTRUMENT

Provenance Presented by the Parish Church of St Michael and All Angels, Stourport-on-Severn, Worcestershire

The organ was made for the parish church of St Michael and All Angels in Stourport-on-Severn, Worcestershire. It was situated at the east end of the south nave aisle. The console was detached and placed behind the south choir stalls, and the bellows were in a chamber below floor level.

When the church closed in 1979, and was subsequently demolished, the organ was dismantled. The pipework was sold for its scrap value, and the console, together with the pedalboard and the various parts of the electric action, were placed temporarily in the Commandery Museum, Worcester.

The organ was presented to Liverpool Museum by St Michael's in 1983, due to the fact that Hope-Jones had lived and worked at Birkenhead on Merseyside.

REFERENCES Sayer, 1981, p.36.
Fox, 1992, p.233.

Free Reed Instruments

Reed Organs

3.1. HARMONIUM, Philip J. Trayser & Co., Stuttgart, *c*.1870

Museum Accession Number 1974.262

Technical specification

Nameboard Inscription	*HarmoniumFabrik. Ph. J. Trayser & Co. Stuttgart*
Retailer's Label	*James Palmer, 34 & 36 Clarence Street, Mount Pleasant, Liverpool*
Compass	4½ Octaves, C – f³, 54 notes
3-Octave-Span	487mm. Bone naturals, stained hardwood sharps
Stops	F Forte S Sourdine E Expression F Forte
Reeds	Brass, one set, brightly voiced
Case Size	Height 852mm, Width 962mm, Depth 488mm
Retailer	James Palmer (1857–*c*.1890)

DESCRIPTION

The plain, rectangular case is of pine, veneered with mahogany, and with some decorative moulding to either side of the lower section. The keycheeks and keyboard surround are both ebonised. The number *17676* is stamped on the top left-hand side of the case. There are two cast-brass carrying handles, one on each side of the case, and a folding mahogany music-stand. The two wooden foot-pedals are covered with carpet which is now very worn.

The stops are placed horizontally above the keyboard on an ebonised ground. The stop-knobs are of porcelain, printed with their values. The Forte stops, for treble and bass, open a wooden flap to increase the sound. The Sourdine stop operates a small wooden cover over the inlet in the valve board, regulating the amount of air admitted and allowing a bass line to be played without dominating the treble line. The Expression stop gives more flexibility and control of sound and allows the flow of air to go directly from the pedals to the reed 'pan', by-passing the reservoir.

Alan Barnes

HISTORY OF THE INSTRUMENT

Provenance   Presented by Mrs Appleby, 1974

volume, while the Vox Humana gives a wavering sound, produced by a revolving fan which causes the air to undulate as it passes over the reeds. The Vox Celeste operates a treble set of reeds, producing a tremolo effect. The Diapason Forte opens the treble flap to increase the volume, while the Dulciana Treble is a half stop, giving a softer sound on the Diapason Treble.

The two pedals are covered with modern, replacement red carpet and have *Doherty Organ* moulded onto the metal plates at the front of each.

Alan Barnes

HISTORY OF THE INSTRUMENT

Provenance Presented by Mr D. Gavin, 1982

This harmonium was bought on hire purchase by the donor's grandfather, at a total cost of £18.18.0, beginning in 1899 and paid over four years.

The maker of this instrument, W. Doherty and Co., began in business around 1875. They grew rapidly in size, manufacturing some 400 organs per month by 1900. In 1908, the firm was renamed the Doherty Piano and Organ Company and, in 1913, the Doherty Piano Company. Upon William Doherty's retirement in 1920 the firm was taken over by Sherlock Manning, a company established in 1902 by John Frank Sherlock and Wilbur Manning, both former employees of Doherty.

ACCORDIONS

3.4. ACCORDION, Busson, Paris, *c.*1860

Museum Accession Number 59.85

Stamp	*Busson, Brevetes, Paris* on the top
	Plain case of ebonised wood, no decoration except for two decorative cast metal braces on underside of keyboard. Small keyboard, the keys capped with ebony and bone. Bellows covered with black paper, embossed with scrolling design.
Dimensions	Height 480mm, width when closed 235mm, depth 180mm
Maker	M. Busson introduced this type of accordion, with small keyboard, in about 1859
Provenance	Presented by Mr D.E. Killender, 1959

3.5. ACCORDION (Flutina), Charles Morris, Tunstall, Staffordshire, *c.*1860–1870

Museum Accession Number 56.97

Label	*Chas. Morris, Musical Inst.t. Maker, High Street, Tunstall* on the bellows Case of ebonised wood, the sides veneered with rosewood inlaid with scrolling floral design in boxwood. Right-hand side inlaid with boxwood stringing. Keys capped with mother-of-pearl. Two long brass keys on the right-hand side and two circular brass keys on the left. Bellows covered with white paper, printed with a floral pattern in green and gold.
Dimensions	Height 378mm, width when closed 155mm, depth 125mm
Maker	A Charles Morris, piano-forte maker, is listed in the Harris, Harrod and Company's Directory and Gazeteer for Tunstall in 1861
Provenance	Purchased from Miss E.G. McVey, 1956

3.6. ACCORDION (Flutina), unsigned, *c.*1860–1880

Museum Accession Number 54.148

Unsigned
Case of ebonised wood, the sides veneered with rosewood and inlaid with scrolling floral patterns in brass, with inlaid swan motifs in bone. Right-hand side inlaid with band of brass in a diamond pattern. Keys capped with intricately carved mother-of-pearl. Two long silver-plated keys on the right-hand side and two circular keys on the left. Bellows covered with silver paper, embossed with scrolling floral design. In own fitted wooden case with sliding lid.

Dimensions   Height 406mm, width when closed 150mm, depth 127mm

Provenance   Presented by Mr and Mrs H.F. Hunt, 1954

3.7. PIANO-ACCORDION, Paolo Soprani, Castelfidardo, Italy, *c.*1920–1930

Museum Accession Number 1989.8.1

Mark — *Soprani, Paolo, Castelfidardo, Italia* in red paint, set with diamante pastes, on the case front
Wooden case, covered with pearlised yellow plastic, set with diamante pastes and edged with bands of black and white checked plastic. Keys capped with plastic, buttons set with diamante pastes. Pierced metal cover next to keyboard, painted red originally and decorated in the centre with a lyre motif. Bellows covered with blue cotton fabric, edged with embossed gold paper. Leather carrying straps.

Dimensions — Height 530mm, width when closed 405mm, depth 190mm

Maker — The firm of Soprani were in business in Castelfidardo, Italy, from at least 1872

Provenance — Presented by Mrs M. Cheetham, 1989

This instrument was bought second-hand by the donor's husband in 1955 from D. Samuels Ltd, 50 Manchester Street, Liverpool for £34.0.0. The firm specialised in the import and sale of piano-accordions and other dance-band instruments

3.8. MELOPHONE, A. Brown, Paris, *c*.1840

Museum Accession Number 1967.161.39

Label	*Exposition 1839, A. Brown, Paris, Rue des Fosses du Temple, 20* on the end
	Guitar-shaped body, the belly of a single piece of sycamore, with two f-shaped soundholes backed with red silk and bordered all around with two lines of inlaid ivory stringing. Body, in two sections, of ebonised wood inlaid with brass stringing and pierced all around sides with c-shaped soundholes. Upper section contains key mechanism, lower section the bellows. Neck and scrolled head also of ebonised wood, with 84 metal buttons in head and vent lever on underside of neck.
Dimensions	Length 750mm, width 280mm, depth 174mm
Maker	A. Brown manufactured melophones for their inventor, the French watchmaker Leclerc, who had first developed the instrument in 1837
Provenance	Paul de Wit, Leipzig, –1922
	Rushworth and Dreaper Ltd, Liverpool, 1922–1967

A note in the archives of Rushworth and Dreaper states that they purchased this instrument from Paul de Wit, on 12th September, 1922, at a cost of £2. Duty and expenses of 16 shillings brought the total cost to £2.16.0.

1.1 Virginals, attributed to Francesco Poggi, Florence, *c.* 1610–1620.

1.1 Virginals, view of soundboard.

1.5 Clavichord, Christian Gottlob Hubert, Anspach, 1783.

2.3 Bottle-Organ, Johann Samuel Kühlewein, Eiseleben, 1798, front view.

2.3 Bottle-Organ, view of bottles from the back.

5.1 Mandore, probably Italian, *c.* 1750–1800, front view.

5.1 Mandore, back view.

5.9   Dital harp, Edward Light, London, *c.* 1818.

5.23 Cither viol, Thomas Perry and William Wilkinson, Dublin, 1792.

5.30 Hurdy-Gurdy, Pierre Tixier, Janzat, France, *c.* 1850–1860, front view.

5.30 Hurdy-Gurdy, detail of peg-box.

7.19   Singing bird automaton, probably Bontems, Paris, *c.* 1900.

Wind Instruments

Woodwind Instruments

4.1. COR ANGLAIS, Jakob Friedrich Grundmann, Dresden, 1791

Museum Accession Number 1967.161.26

Stamp *Grundmann*, below crossed swords, on the top and middle joints, and *Grundmann, Dresden, 1791*, below crossed swords on the bell.

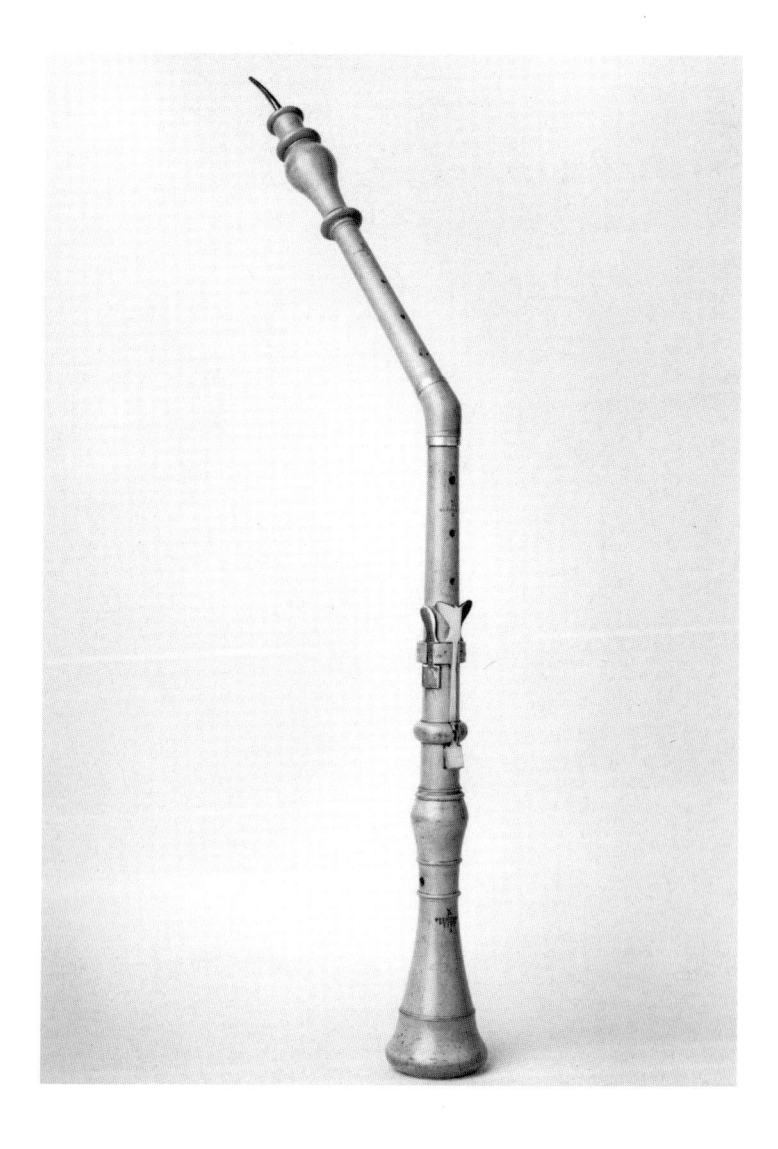

Angular form. Three main joints of unstained maple with a boxwood knee and two brass mounts. The joints comprise a turned onion and cotton reel finial with curved brass crook; the upper joint; a short, obtuse-angled knee-joint; the lower joint and the bell section of turned baluster-shape. Two square brass keys are mounted on turned, raised wooden sections, one of them a fish-tailed F key, the other a right hand G# key. Both key pads are of leather. Pitch of the instrument : F.

Dimensions Length of top section 355mm, length of lower section 495mm, bore diameter 5.9mm at socket expanding to 23mm before bell chamber.

Maker Jakob Friedrich Grundmann (*c.*1727–1800), studied instrument making in Leipzig under Johann Poerschman. He established his workshop in Dresden around 1744, specialising in the making of oboes. Most of his instruments are stamped with the year of manufacture on the bell.

Provenance Charles van Raalte, Brownsea Island, Dorset, –1925
Sir Arthur Wheeler, Brownsea Island, Dorset, 1925–1927
Rushworth and Dreaper Ltd, Liverpool, 1927–1967

Rushworth and Dreaper purchased this instrument from Sir Arthur Wheeler of Brownsea Castle, Brownsea Island, Dorset, on 21st June, 1927, for the sum of £1.17.6. It had been part of the collection formed by the Castle's previous owner, Charles van Raalte, who bought Brownsea Island in 1901. Sir Arthur bought the island, the castle and its contents from him in 1925 but was forced to sell everything in 1927 due to bankruptcy.

References Sale catalogue, Fox and Sons, 1927, pp.103, 107, lot 1760.
Baines, 1966, p.105, fig.577.
Spiegl, 1972, pp.43, 49.
Whittington-Egan, 1976, p.157.
Young, 1978, p.128.
Bevan, 1990. p.68.

4.2. FLUTE, D'Almaine and Co., London, *c.*1800

Museum Accession Number 1967.161.25

Stamp *D'Almaine & Co., late Goulding & D'Almaine, Soho Square, London* on the top joint, and *D'Almaine & Co.* across the Prince of Wales' feathers, on the two middle joints.

Boxwood, in four joints, with three ivory mounts and later replacement mount of nickel silver on head joint. One square nickel silver key in the foot joint. Pitch of the instrument : D + 40 cents.

Dimensions Overall length 598mm, length from centre of mouth-hole to foot 531mm, bore of head joint 16.4mm, bore of foot 13.4mm.

Maker The firm of D'Almaine and Co. existed between 1798 and 1866. They specialised in the making of woodwind and brass instruments, and were based at a number of addresses in London. This instrument was probably made at their premises at 45 Pall Mall, which they occupied from 1798 until 1806, or possibly at their other premises at 76 St James's Street, occupied from 1800–1806.

Provenance Rushworth and Dreaper Ltd, Liverpool, 1936–1967

A record in Rushworth and Dreaper's archives states that this instrument was 'presented to Mr W. Maynard Rushworth in 1936', but does not give the name of the donor.

4.3. FLUTE, Freeman, London, *c.* 1830–1834

Museum Accession Number 56.38

Stamp — *Freeman, London* on three joints.

Rosewood, in five joints, with seven nickel silver mounts. Eight circular nickel silver keys, the lower two with pewter plugs, all mounted on wooden saddles. The mouth-hole is bushed with ivory with three inlaid brass repair pins at either side. Metal-sleeved tuning barrel. Replacement cap in head joint. Pitch of the instrument: D.

In a black leather-covered case, lined with red velvet, with silver lid-plate inscribed *Harvey Ludlow, 26th Feby. 1845*.

Dimensions — Overall length 669mm, length from centre of mouth-hole to foot 590mm, bore of head joint 17.8mm, bore of foot 10.8mm.

Maker — The firm of Freeman of London was in business between 1815 and 1834, suggesting that the case and instrument may not be contemporary. The instrument is not an exact fit for the case.

Provenance — Purchased from Mr R. Thompson, 1956.

4.4. CLARINET, Clementi and Co., London, *c*.1810

Museum Accession Number 1970.42

Stamp *Clementi & Compy. No. 26 Cheapside, London, G.Miller Fecit* on the top joint, *Clementi & Compy* on the three middle joints, and *Clementi & Compy. No. 26 Cheapside, London,* on the bell.

Boxwood, in five joints, with six ivory mounts. Original mouthpiece in boxwood with long tuning tenon. Six square brass keys mounted on wooden saddles. Pitch of the instrument : C.

Dimensions Overall length, including mouthpiece 613mm, main bore diameter 13.8mm.

Maker The firm of Clementi and Co. was established by the Italian musician, Muzio Clementi (1752–1832), in 1798, in partnership with John Longman, Frederick William Collard, Frederick Augustus Hyde, Josiah Banger and David Davis. Initially, from 1798 until 1800, they occupied the former Cheapside premises of the firm of Longman & Broderip. After Longman left in 1800 to set up on his own, they became known as Clementi and Co. Various other name-changes occured until Clementi's death in 1832, when the firm became known as Collard and Collard.

Clementi and Co. specialised in the manufacture of pianos and in the sale of sheet-music. It is unclear whether they actually manufactured the woodwind instruments stamped with their name or if they simply retailed them for other makers.

Provenance Purchased from Sotheby's, 27th November, 1969, lot 4.

References Sale catalogue, Sotheby and Co., 27th November, 1969, p.5, lot 4.

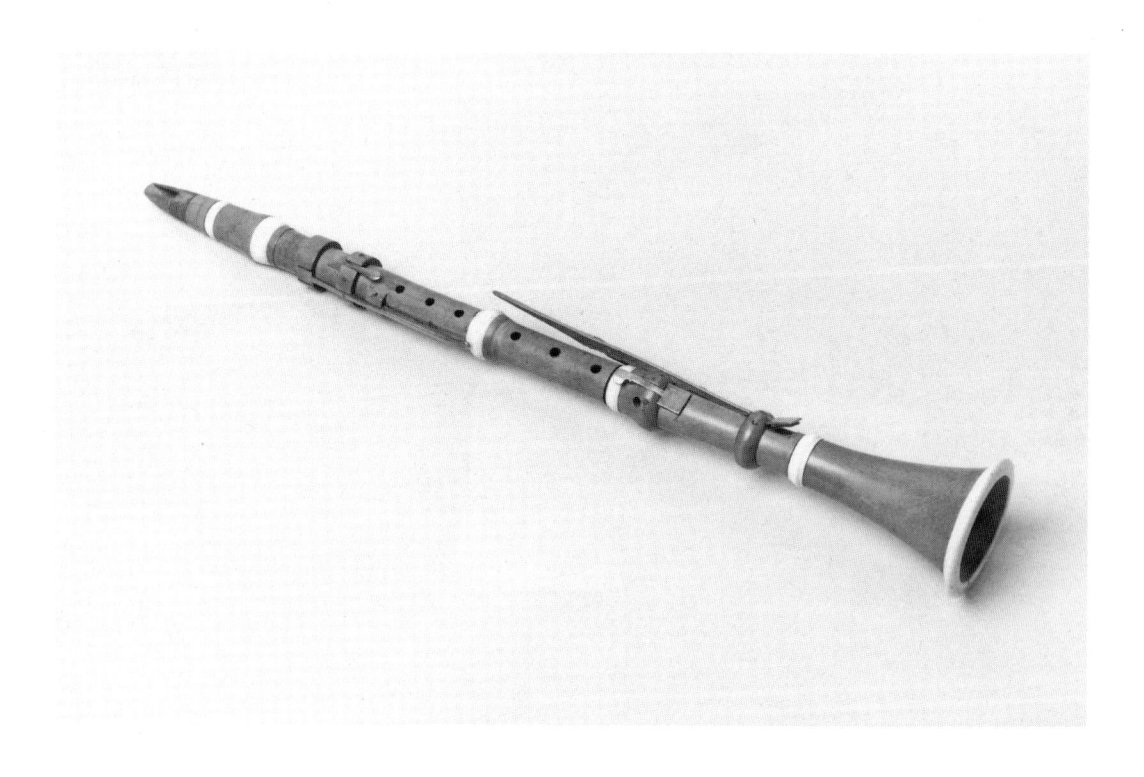

4.5. CLARINET, Jordan, Liverpool, *c*.1810

Museum Accession Number WAG 1993.67

Stamp — *Jordan, Liverpool*, with a star above and crown below, on top and bell joint, and *Jordan, Liverpool*, with a crown below, on the middle joint.

Stained boxwood, in four joints, with ebony mouthpiece and three original ivory mounts. Barrel and mouthpiece are modern reconstructions (1993) for display purposes. Middle joint of a lighter colour and with different stamp, suggesting that it may be a later replacement. Eight circular brass keys, mounted on wooden saddles, six original, two reconstruction (1993) for display purposes. Pitch of the instrument : B flat.

Dimensions — Length of original three joints 543mm, length of reconstructed barrel and mouthpiece 116mm, main bore diameter 13.3mm.

Maker — The family firm of Jordan was established in 1830, by James Jordan, at 24 Manchester Street, Liverpool. They specialised in the manufacture and sale of brass and woodwind instruments and continued in business until about 1930. This instrument was probably made by an earlier, unknown maker and received Jordan's stamp when sold by them. It resembles the work of Thomas Key, a well-known maker of woodwind instruments, active from *c*.1800–*c*.1840.

Provenance — Presented by Mr Fritz Spiegl, 1970.

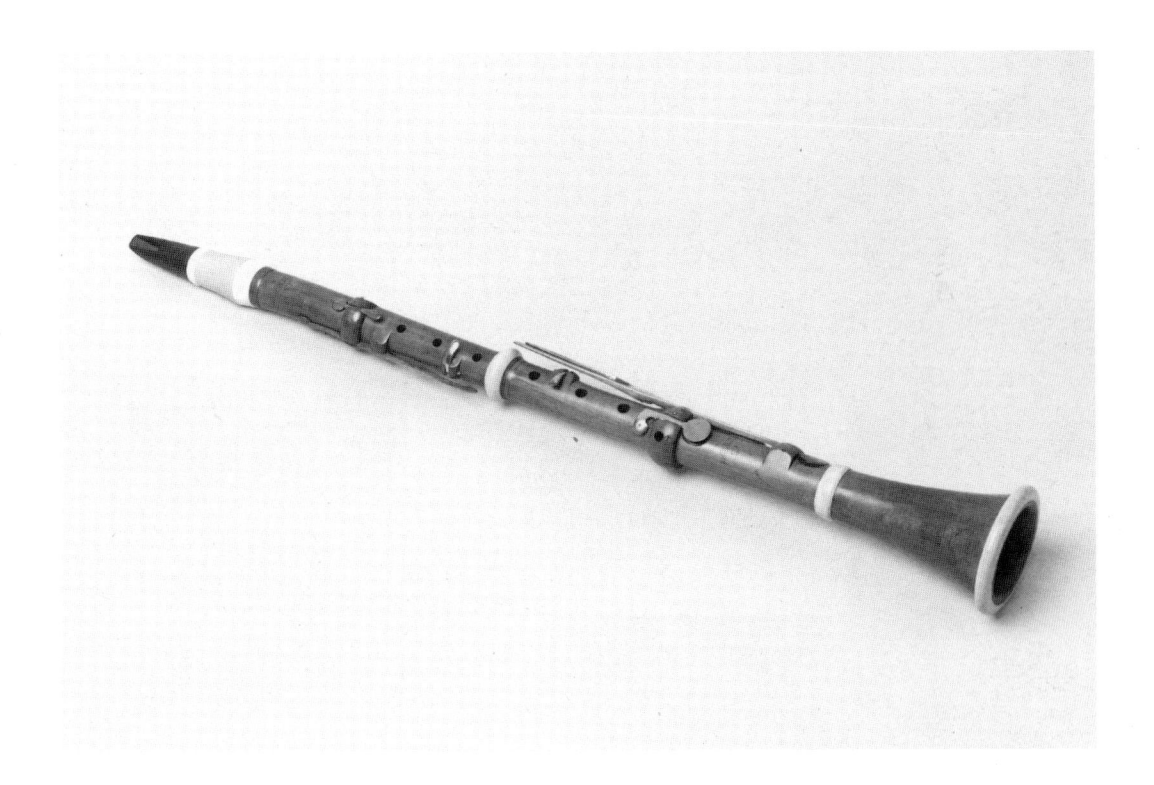

4.6. CLARINET, Metzler and Co., London, *c.*1840

Museum Accession Number 1970.96

Stamp *Metzler & Co., London*, on all three joints and on the bell, and *Metzler* on the reed cover.

Boxwood, in four joints, with three brass mounts, the lower barrel mount, thumb rest and the bell mount now missing. Original ebony mouthpiece. Rosewood reed cover with brass mount missing. Thirteen circular brass keys mounted on pillars. Pitch of the instrument : B flat.

Dimensions Overall length 643mm, main bore diameter 14.3mm.

Maker The firm of Metzler and Co. was founded in London in 1788 by the German instrument maker Valentin Metzler (d. *c.*1833). In 1816 Valentin's son, George Metzler, joined the firm and they became known as Metzler and Son. In 1833, upon the death of Valentin, the firm changed its name again to G. Metzler and Co.

Provenance Presented by Mr G.W. George, 1970.

4.7. DOUBLE FLAGEOLET, Clementi and Co., London, c.1800–1810

Museum Accession Number 52.47

Stamp *Patent, Clementi & Co., London*, on head joint and on main body joint.

Boxwood, in five joints plus mouthpiece, consisting of two chanters of equal length set in a common stock, surmounted by a two-piece wind cap. Windcap top and mouthpiece are modern reconstructions (1993) for display purposes. Five original ivory mounts and three original studs. Seven square silver keys mounted on wooden saddles. Two long, silver cut-off keys on the common stock. The left-hand chanter has two keys and a block for a third, now missing. The right-hand chanter has three keys on the front and another at the back. The finger holes and keys have their pitches stamped beside them. Pitch of the instrument : D.

Dimensions Length of original instrument 333mm, length of reconstructed top section 62mm, bore at tenons 11.5mm, bore at feet 10mm.

Provenance Presented by Mr Thomas Best, 1952.

This instrument was given to the donor as a boy, around 1880, by the Hon. Alfred Cookson, Rector of Kirkby Thore Parish Church, Cumbria, although there is no evidence that it was ever played in the church.

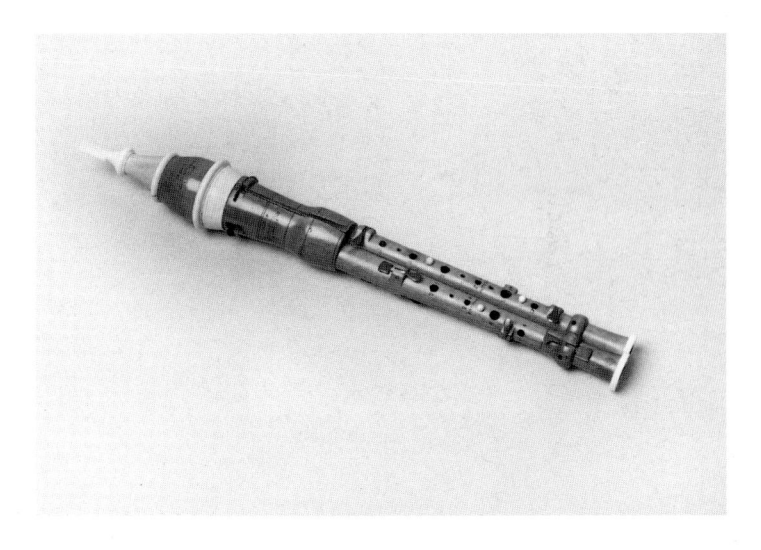

4.8. DOUBLE FLAGEOLET, William Bainbridge, London, c.1800–1808

Museum Accession Number 1967.161.24c

Stamp — *Bainbridge Inventor, Holburn Hill, London* on the top joint, and *Bainbridge Inventor, 35 Holburn Hill, London, New Patent*, on main body joint and on the bottom of the right-hand chanter.

Boxwood, in six joints, plus mouthpiece, consisting of two chanters of unequal length set in a common stock, surmounted by a two-piece windcap. Six ivory mounts, four studs and mouthpiece. Fifteen square silver keys mounted on wooden saddles, four being later matching additions. Two long silver cut-off keys on the stock. Silver band around stock. The left-hand chanter has seven keys (two of them additions), and the right-hand chanter has seven keys (two of them additions), and a 'New C Key' for the left hand on the stock. The finger holes and keys have their pitches stamped beside them. Pitch of the instrument : D.

Dimensions — Overall length 536mm, overall length of left-hand chanter 267mm, overall length of right-hand chanter 322mm, bore at tenons 15mm, bore at right foot 10mm, bore at left foot 11mm.

Maker — William Bainbridge (d. c.1831), produced woodwind instruments, especially flageolets, between c.1800 and c.1830. From c.1808–1820, the firm was known as Bainbridge and Wood. After Bainbridge's death, the firm was continued, until 1835, by his widow and subsequently, until 1855, by his partner Hastrick.

Provenance — Rushworth and Dreaper Ltd, Liverpool, 1956–1967.

A record in the archives of Rushworth and Dreaper states that they purchased this instrument on 6th November, 1956, from Ernest W. Thompson, of Tullymore School, Broughshane, Co. Antrim, Northern Ireland, for the sum of £5.5.0.

References — Spiegl, 1972, p. 43.

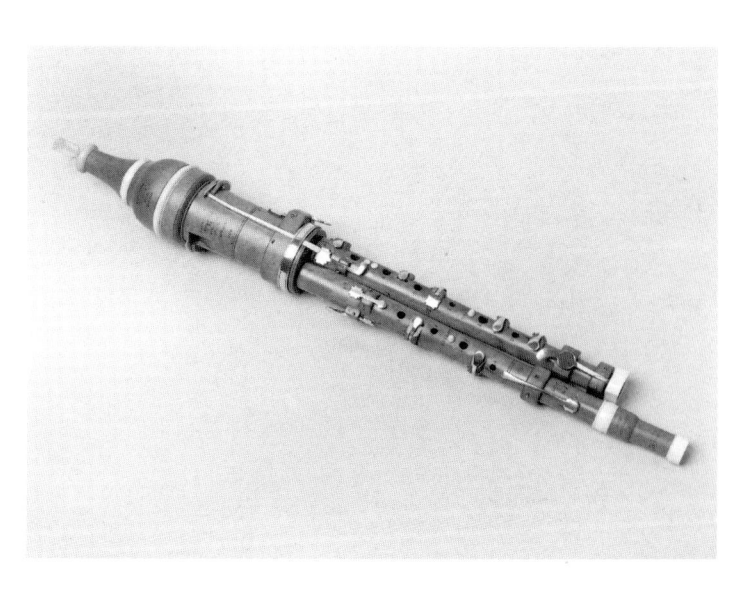

4.9. DOUBLE FLAGEOLET, Bainbridge and Wood, London, *c*.1808–1820

Museum Accession Number 1967.161.24a

Stamp *Bainbridge Inventor, Holburn Hill, London*, below a crown, on the top joint, and *Bainbridge & Wood, 35 Holburn Hill, London, Patent*, on the main body joint.

Boxwood, in five joints, mouthpiece missing, consisting of two chanters of equal length set in a common stock, surmounted by a two-piece windcap. Six ivory mounts and eight studs. The ivory foot mount on the right-hand chanter has a section missing from the back. Five square, silver keys and two long silver cut-off keys on the stock. The left-hand chanter has two keys, and the right-hand chanter three. The finger holes and keys have their pitches stamped beside them. Pitch of the instrument : C.

Dimensions Overall length 460mm, bore at tenons 14.5mm, bore at feet 10.5mm.

Provenance Rushworth and Dreaper Ltd, Liverpool, –1967.

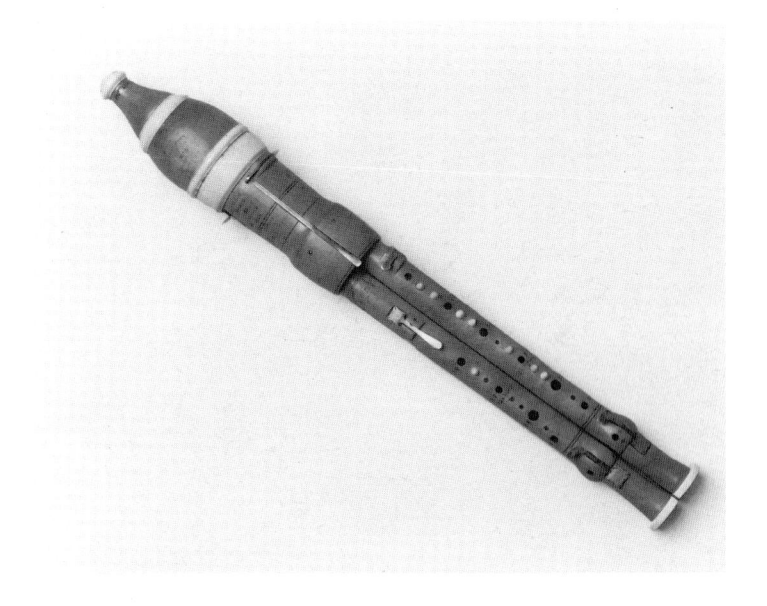

4.10. DOUBLE FLAGEOLET, Bainbridge and Wood, London, *c.*1808–1820

Museum Accession Number 1967.161.24b

Stamp *Bainbridge, Inventor, Holborn Hill, London*, below a crown, on the top joint, and *Bainbridge & Wood, 35 Holborn Hill, London, Patent*, on the main body joint.

Boxwood, in five joints, plus mouthpiece, consisting of two chanters of equal length set in a common stock, surmounted by a two-piece windcap. Six ivory mounts and fourteen studs. Four square silver keys and one square brass replacement key. Two long silver cut-off keys on the stock. The left-hand chanter has two keys, one a replacement, and the right-hand chanter has three keys. The finger holes and keys have their pitches stamped beside them. Pitch of the instrument : C.

Dimensions Overall length 495mm, bore at tenons 16mm, bore at feet 11mm.

Provenance Rushworth and Dreaper Ltd, Liverpool, –1967.

References Spiegl, 1972, p.43.

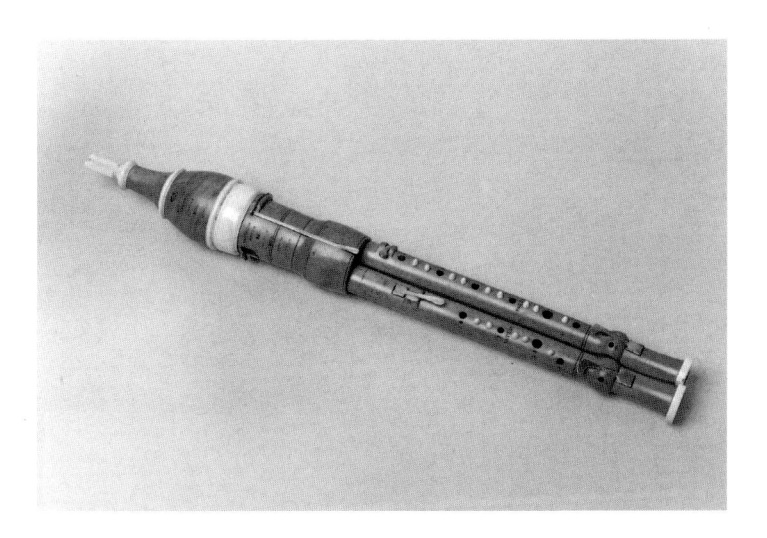

4.11. DOUBLE FLAGEOLET, Bainbridge and Wood, London, *c*.1808–1820

Museum Accession Number 59.6

Stamp *Bainbridge, Inventor, Holborn Hill, London, Holborn*, on the top joint, and *Bainbridge & Wood, 35 Holborn Hill, London, Patent*, below a crown, on the main body joint.

Boxwood, in five joints, plus modern reconstruction mouthpiece (1993), consisting of two chanters of equal length set in a common stock, surmounted by a two-piece windcap. Six ivory mounts and ten studs. Five square silver keys and two long silver cut-off keys on the stock. The left-hand chanter has two keys and the right-hand chanter three. The finger holes and keys have their pitches stamped beside them. Pitch of the instrument : D.

Dimensions Overall length, including reconstructed mouthpiece 404mm, bore at tenons 11mm, bore at feet 7mm.

Provenance Purchased from Mr F.B. Bromley, 1959.

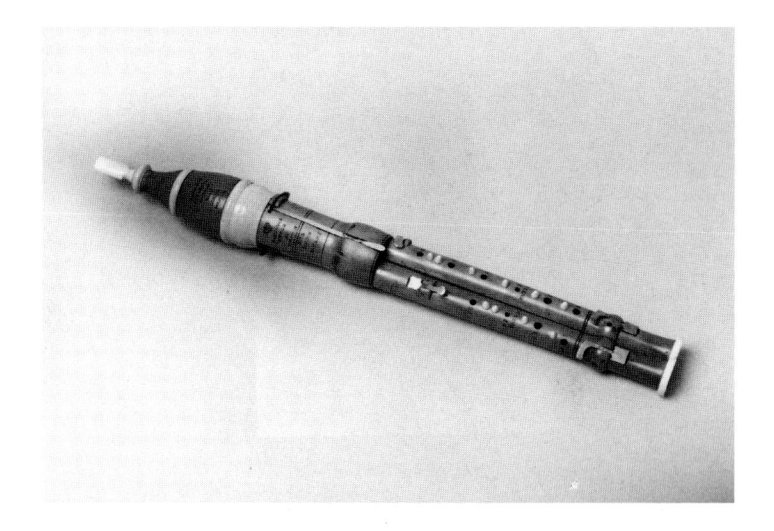

4.12. FIFE, Henry Potter, London, *c*.1905–1910

Museum Accession Number 1966.58

Stamp *Hy. Potter & Co., London*, on the head joint, and *Hy. Potter & Co. 35 & 38 West Street, Charing Road, London*, on the main body joint.

African blackwood, in two joints, with three nickel silver mounts. Five circular nickel silver keys in wooden mounts. Pitch of the instrument : B.
In own brown leather case, for attachment to a belt, with *W.L.J. 50th Batt. Band 3854*, scratched on the back, and *3854 W.L. Jenkin* scratched on one side.

Dimensions Overall length 387mm, length from centre of mouth-hole to foot 317mm, bore of head joint 12.7mm, bore of foot 9mm.

Maker The firm of Henry Potter and Co. was established in 1904 and is still in business today, trading from West Street, Charing Cross Road, London. They specialised in instruments for military bands, especially drums and woodwind instruments.

Provenance Presented by Mrs L.J. Parry, 1966.

4.13. FIFE, Ward and Sons, Liverpool, *c*.1870–1890

Museum Accession Number 1972.246.25a

Stamp *Ward & Sons, 10 St Anne St., Liverpool*, on top and bottom joints, and *Ward & Son, Liverpool*, on the middle joint.

Ebony, in three joints, all the mounts now missing. Four circular silver-plated keys, mounted on metal pillars. Metal-sleeved sliding tuning-barrel, with cork stopper, in the head joint. Pitch of the instrument : B flat.

Dimensions Overall length 388mm, length from centre of mouth-hole to foot 328mm, bore of head joint 12.7mm, bore of foot 10.5mm.

Maker The firm of Ward's was established in 1803 by Cornelius Ward, in Lord Street, Liverpool. He moved to Church Street around 1806, where he remained until 1811 when he moved to London. Cornelius' sons, Roger and Richard J. Ward appear to have carried on the business in Liverpool after their father left the city. Between 1870 and the early 1930s, when the firm finally went out of business, Richard J. Ward and his sons were based at 10 St Anne Street, Liverpool, and this was the period of the firm's greatest growth and prosperity. They specialised in the making and retailing of military and brass band instruments, and in importing instruments from abroad.

Provenance Presented by Miss M. Moston, 1972.

4.14. PICCOLO, unsigned, c.1870–1890

Museum Accession Number 1972.246.25b.

Unsigned.

Ebony, in three joints, with two nickel silver mounts. Two of the mounts are now missing and the remaining two both have pieces missing. Six circular silver-plated keys, mounted on metal pillars. Metal-sleeved sliding tuning-barrel, with cork stopper, in the head joint. Pitch of the instrument : D.

Dimensions   Overall length 310mm, length from centre of mouth-hole to foot 257mm, bore of head joint 10.4mm, bore of foot 7.6mm.

Provenance   Presented by Miss M. Moston, 1972.

4.15. TREBLE RECORDER, attributed to Arnold Dolmetsch, London, *c*.1920–1930

Museum Accession Number 1982.9

Unsigned.

Rosewood, in three joints, with pencil cedar plug. Seven simple fingerholes and one thumb hole. Pitch of the instrument : E –30 cents. In own rectangular wooden box.

Dimensions — Overall length 504mm, speaking length 450mm, bore diameter at head joint 28.8mm, bore at foot 11mm.

Maker — Arnold Dolmetsch (1858–1940) usually stamped his wind instruments *Dolmetsch*. The fact that this example is unmarked suggests that it was a prototype from his workshop.

Provenance — Presented by Mrs V. Yorke, 1979.

4.16. BASSOON, unsigned, Bohemia, *c*.1850

Museum Accession Number 1967.161.22

Unsigned.

Figured maple covered with dark brown varnish, in five joints (wing joint consists of two parts) with five brass mounts. Twelve circular brass keys (and one now missing) mounted on brass saddles. The bell end has been repaired and the tuning slide in the wing joint shortened. The two octave keys are fitted with adjustable slides. Curved brass crook. Owner's initials, V.F., on boot joint in brass nails. Pitch of the instrument : F.

Dimensions Height 1222mm, bore at socket 12.5mm, bore at long joint tenon 23.6mm, bore at bell 31mm.

Provenance Rushworth and Dreaper Ltd, Liverpool, 1923–1967.

A record in the archives of Rushworth and Dreaper states that they purchased this instrument from (the dealers ?) Fuchs and Wollner on 28th May 1923, for the sum of 35 shillings. With (import ?) duty added the total cost was £2.7.5.

References R & D catalogue 1 (undated), not paginated.
R & D catalogue 2 (undated), p.9, p.10 (two editions).

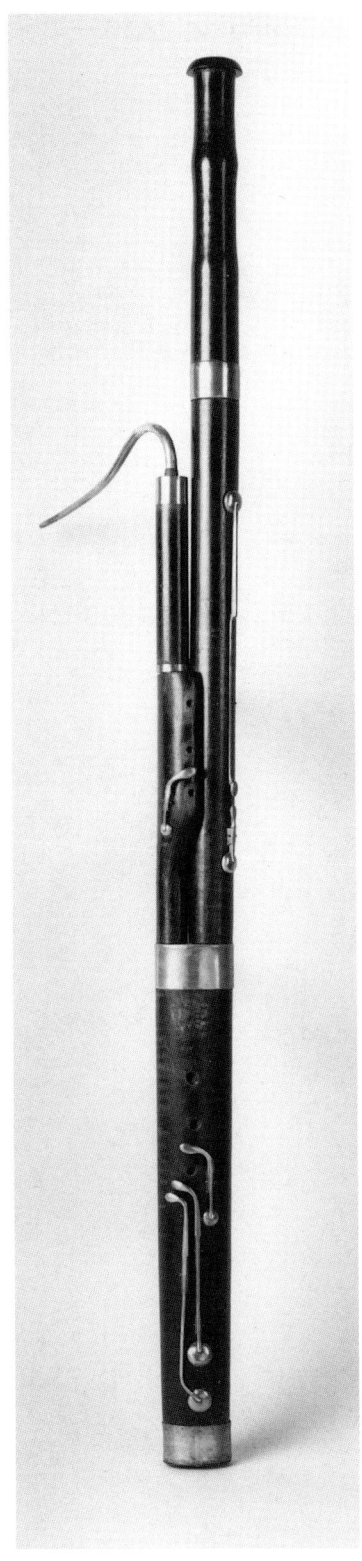

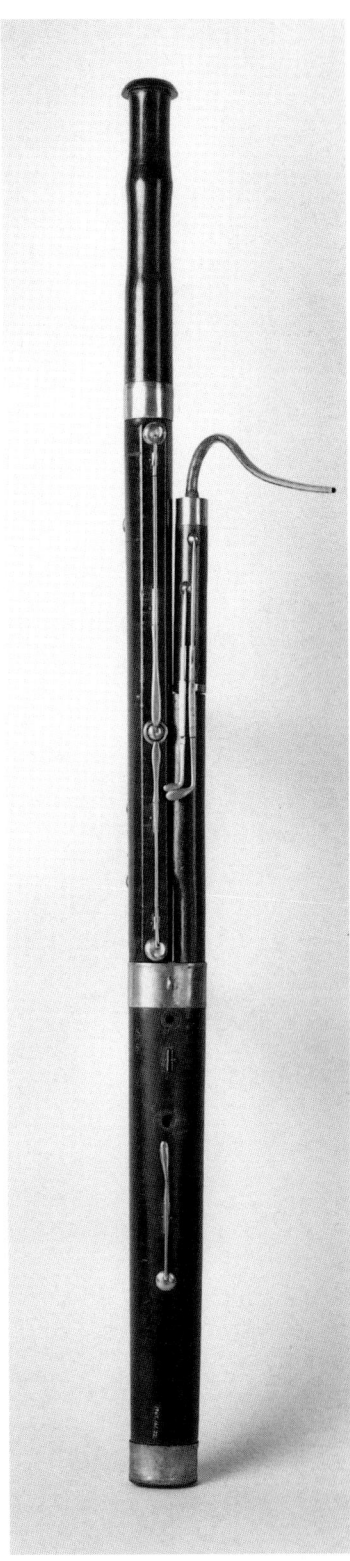

Front view   Back view

4.17. BASSOON, Hawkes and Son, *c*.1900–1910

Museum Accession Number WAG 1993.68

Stamp Hawkes and Son, Denman Street, Piccadilly Circus, London, 31 very faintly on wing joint and boot. Owner's stamp of *T. Bartlett* appears at random all over the instrument.

Rosewood, in four joints, with five nickel-silver mounts. Sixteen circular nickel-silver keys, mounted on pillars with rods and axles. The crook is now missing. Instrument shows signs of heavy use, with wear around the finger holes, wax in the holes for tuning and additional springs and repairs to the keywork. Pitch of the instrument: F (high pitch).

In own black leather travelling case, including pouch and box in the lid for reeds, stamped *Hawkes and Son, Denman St, Piccadilly Circus, London W*, inside the lid, the lettering in the style of the period *c.*1900–1910.

Dimensions Height 1268mm, bore at socket 13.5mm, bore at long joint tenon 25mm, bore at bell 42mm.

Maker The firm of Hawkes and Son was established in 1884, specialising in wind instruments. They amalgamated with the firm of Boosey and Co. in 1930, becoming Boosey and Hawkes, the name under which they still trade today.

Provenance Unknown.

Front view
Back view

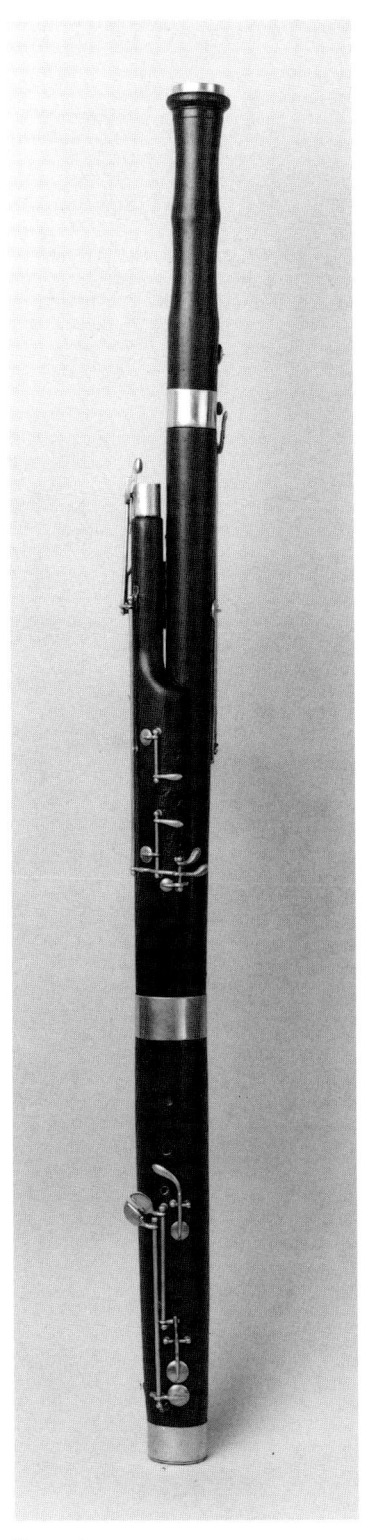

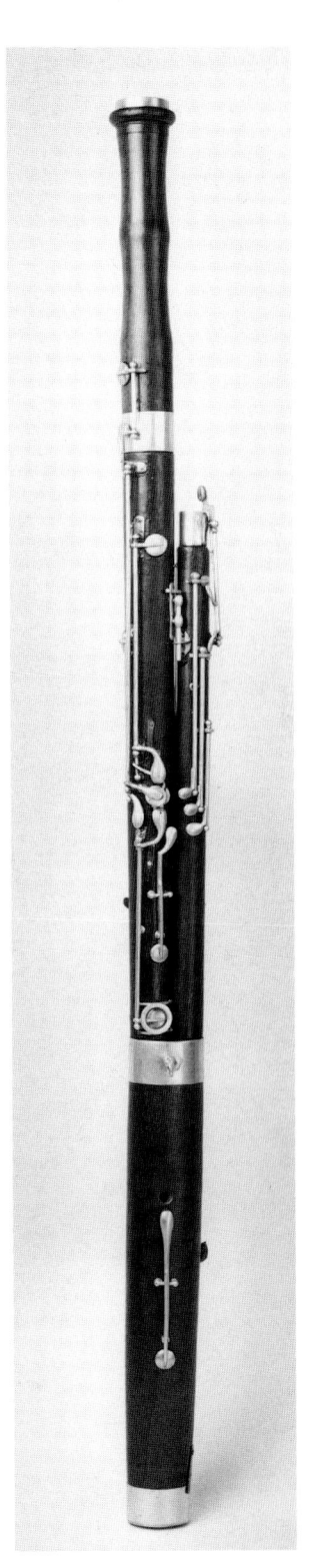

4.18. SERPENT, unsigned, early nineteenth century

Museum Accession Number 57.165

Unsigned.

Serpentine-shaped body of wood, covered originally with black leather, the curves supported by five brass braces. Leather replaced in the 1970s, during conservation, by some form of black tape. Six fingerholes, five bushed with ivory, one with bone. Five circular brass keys originally, one now completely missing and two having lost their tails. Brass mounts on the mouthpiece end and bell. Original brass crook and mouthpiece now missing. Some evidence of red paint inside the bell.

Dimensions Height 773mm, tube length 2460mm, diameter of bell 110mm.

Provenance Purchased from John Maggs Antiques, 114 Bold Street, Liverpool, 1957, for £26.0.0.

This instrument is said to have been played in an unnamed church in Derby.

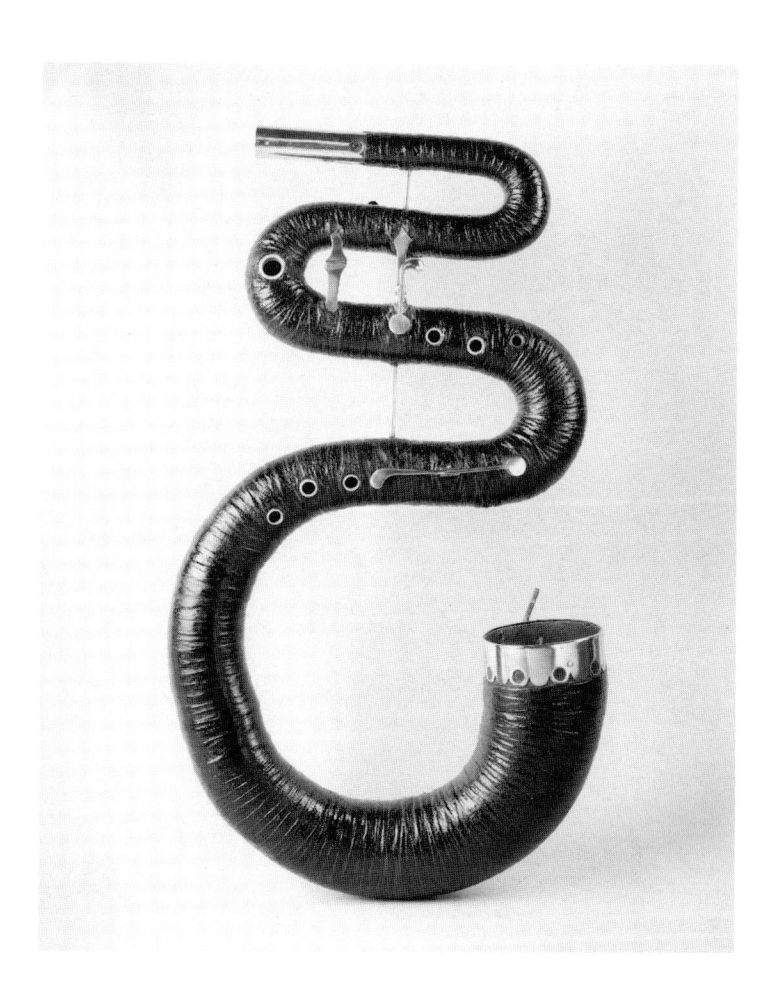

4.19. SERPENT, John Fusedale, Westminster, early nineteenth century

Museum Accession Number 1967.161.20

Inscription *Jn. Fusedale, 14 Dartmouth St, Westminster* on the mouthpiece end.

Serpentine-shaped body of wood covered with black leather, the curves supported by six brass braces. Bell mount and mouthpiece end of brass, the original brass crook and mouthpiece now missing. Replacement brass and ivory mouthpiece. Six fingerholes bushed with ivory and six circular keys.

4.21. BAGPIPES, (Half-Long Pipes), James Robertson, Edinburgh, *c.*1930s

Museum Accession Number 63.229

Stamp *Robertson, Edinburgh* on the mouthpiece.

Rosewood pipes, the original chanter broken off near the mount and a modern reconstruction (1993) fitted. Three drones of rosewood, all mounted with a synthetic resin, possibly an early plastic. Bag of rubberised canvas, covered with green and black checked wool plaid, trimmed with red and green wool fringing. Bellows of ash and leather, with iron bracket and synthetic ivory mount. Bellows probably not original match with bag and pipes.

Dimensions Length of reconstructed chanter 330mm, visible length of longest drone, excluding stock, 405mm, visible length of shortest drone 295mm.

Provenance Presented by Mrs Simey, 1963.

Brass Instruments

4.22. HUNTING HORN, early-mid nineteenth century

Museum Accession Number M5110

Unsigned.

Made from one single coil of brass, with integral, cup-shaped mouthpiece of brass. The curled edge of the bell rim is now split and damaged. Pitch of the instrument : E flat.

Dimensions Length 160mm, diameter of bell 75mm.

Provenance Presented by Joseph Mayer, 1867.

4.23. KEY BUGLE, Charles Pace, Westminster, *c.*1830

Museum Accession Number 1967.161.23

Stamp   *Charles Pace, No.2 Crown Street, Westminster* on the bell rim.

Copper, with brass mounts. A section of the tube, the mouthpiece and the applied bell rim are also of brass. Seven circular brass keys mounted on brass saddles. Rim of the mouthpiece of nickel silver. Pitch of the instrument : C with extension crook to B flat.

Dimensions   Length 562mm, diameter of bell 160mm.

Maker   The brothers Frederick and Charles Pace worked together at 2 Lower Crown Street, London, between 1830 and 1834. They specialised in the manufacture of keyed bugles and slide trumpets.

Provenance   Rushworth and Dreaper Ltd, Liverpool, 1925–1967.

A record in the archives of Rushworth and Dreaper states that they purchased this instrument 'over the counter' in 1925 for the sum of £1.10.0.

References   R & D catalogue 1 (undated), not paginated.

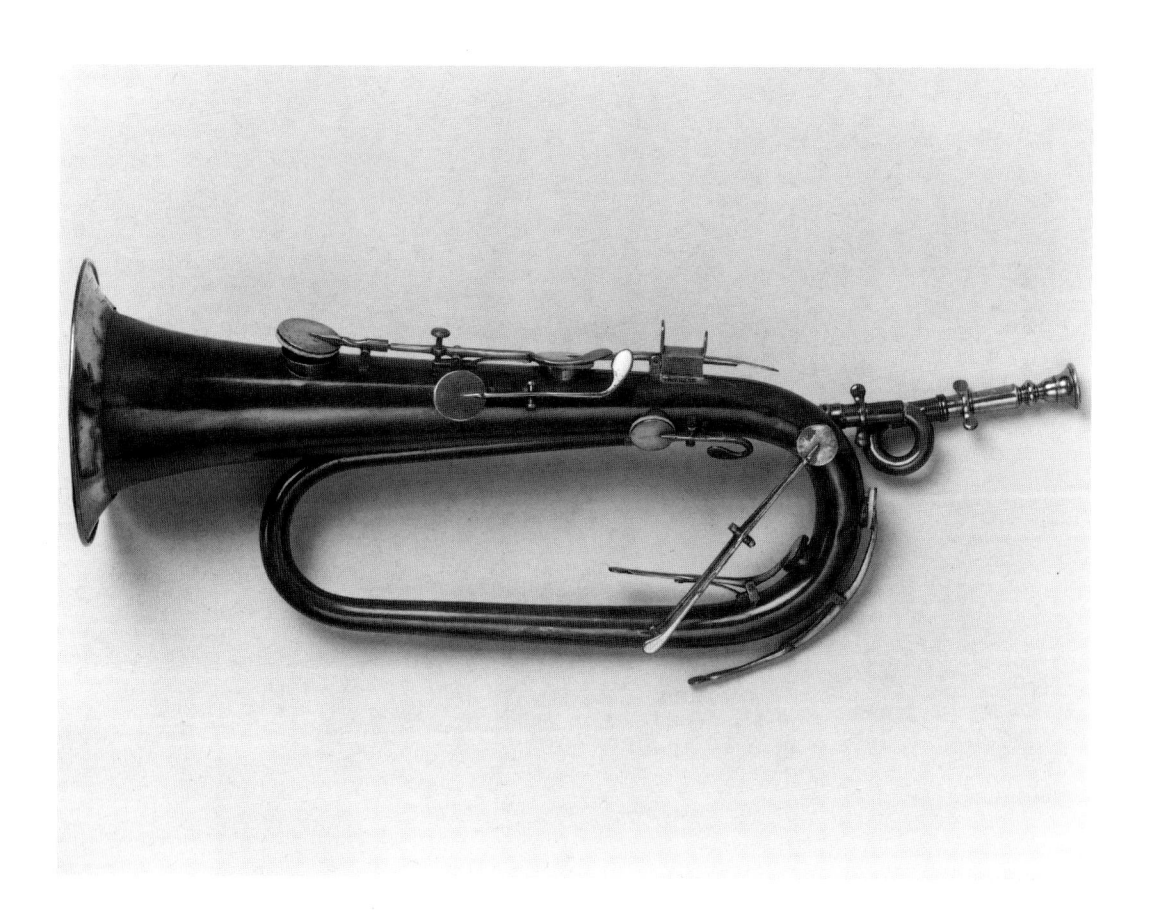

4.24. BUGLE, Russian, *c*.1850–1860

Museum Accession Number 50.17.7

Stamp *Regezer (illegible) Peterburg* on the bell rim.

Made from a single coil of brass, with cup-shaped brass mouthpiece. Patinated brass bell rim, and embossed and patinated oval cartouche, worked with a double-headed eagle against two crossed anchors, below a crown. Mouthpiece not original. Pitch of the instrument : C.

Dimensions Length 235mm, diameter of bell 82mm.

Provenance Presented by Mrs S. Lade, 1950.
　This instrument is said to have been used at the siege of Sebastopol in 1856.

4.25. VALVE BUGLE, (Bersaglieri horn), Romeo Orsi, Milan, *c.*1885–1890

Museum Accession Number 1967.161.27

Stamp *Ditta, Prof. Romeo Orsi, Trade Mark, Milano-Italia, Mod.1884* on the bell rim.

Brass, with single piston valve and brass cup-shaped mouthpiece. Pitch of the instrument : B flat modulating to F.

Dimensions Length 393mm, diameter of bell 100mm.

Provenance Rushworth and Dreaper Ltd, Liverpool, 1958–1967.

A record in the archives of Rushworth and Dreaper states that this instrument was presented to them by the Small Goods department in September 1958.

4.26. OPHICLEIDE, Pollard, Wibsey, Bradford, *c*.mid nineteenth century

Museum Accession Number 1967.161.21

Stamp *Pollard, Maker, Wibsey, Nr. Bradford* on the bell rim.

Brass, with two silver mounts on the crook. Eleven circular brass keys mounted on brass saddles. The cup-shaped mouthpiece is now missing. Pitch of the instrument : C.

Dimensions Height 1090mm, diameter of bell 190mm.

Maker John Pollard, musical instrument maker, is listed in Bradford's local trade directories between 1837 and 1847. During that period, he was based in North Bierley, to the south of the city. Wibsey was part of the township of North Bierley until 1899.

Provenance Rushworth and Dreaper Ltd, Liverpool, 1925–1967.

A record in the archives of Rushworth and Dreaper states that they purchased this instrument on 31st October, 1925, from 'Baggaly, Manchester', for the sum of £4.10.0. Cecil Baggaley, of 7 Regent Road, Manchester, was a dealer in musical instruments.

References Weston, 1989, pp. 130–133.

4.27. OPHICLEIDE, R.J. Ward, Liverpool, 1848

Museum Accession Number 57.114

Inscription *R.J. Ward, Maker, 57 Sir Thomas Buildings, Liverpool A.D.1848*, on an engraved ribbon entwined with palm leaves, and *Ward's, Liverpool*, on a cartouche.

Copper, with nickel-silver mounts and keys, and applied and embossed garland decorated with musical instruments, animals and scrolling motifs. There is an applied nickel silver shield, surmounted by the Liver Bird, above the name inscription. Decorative silver boot, cast and applied, with scrolling floral decoration. Eleven circular nickel silver keys, mounted on nickel silver bridges, the head of each key decorated with engine-turned designs. Ivory cup-shaped mouthpiece. Pitch of the instrument : C.

Dimensions Height 1100mm, diameter of bell 210mm.

Provenance Presented by Mrs Muriel Ward, 1957.

References Spiegl, 1972, p.49.
Weston, 1983, pp.109–110.
Weston, 1989, pp.130–133.
Bevan, 1990, p.68.

Detail

4.28. PAIR OF TRUMPETS, London, 1908

Museum Accession Number 46.69.45a & b

Inscription *Sir William Henry Tate Bart., High Sheriff of Lancashire, 1907 & 1908* on each bell.

Silver, stamped with the London assay mark for 1908, and the maker's mark, D.K. G.K., in a square cartouche, on the bells, the bell rims, the tubes and the mouthpieces. The bell rims are embossed with stylised floral decoration. The applied mounts and knops on the tubes are also decorated with embossed, stylised motifs. Pitch of the instruments : E flat.

Each with a blue silk trumpet banner, painted with the arms of Tate.

Dimensions	Length 683mm, diameter of bell 120mm.
Provenance	Presented by Lieutenant Colonel Sir Henry Tate, Bt., 1946.

William Henry Tate (1842–1921), was the eldest son of Sir Henry Tate (1819–1899), founder of the Liverpool-based sugar-refining business of Tate and Lyle.

4.29. SLIDE TRUMPET, F.J. Lee, London, 1914

Museum Accession Number 1975.89

Inscription *Class A, F.J. Lee, Military Band Instrument Manufacturer, London, E, 14057, Harry Allen (Patentee)* on the bell.

Silver plate on copper alloy, in two sections, with long sliding copper alloy tube. The bell is decorated with engraved roses. Cup-shaped silver-plated mouthpiece, stamped *Besson & Co., Prototype*. Pitch of the instrument : B flat.

Dimensions Total length 1150mm, length of the slide, to mouthpiece 715mm, diameter of bell 118mm.

Maker Frederick John Lee was in business as a maker and seller of military musical instruments from about 1910 until 1924. Working first from 2a Whitehead Street, Mile End Road, by 1914 he had moved to 62 Buckhurst Street, Bethnal Green where he remained in business until 1924.

Provenance Presented by Mrs S. Skelhorn, 1975.

This instrument was designed and made for the donor's father, Henry Allen, a professional musician in Liverpool before the First World War, who worked under the name of Harry Fisher. The design was registered at the Patent Office on 27th March, 1914 as Patent number 634639.

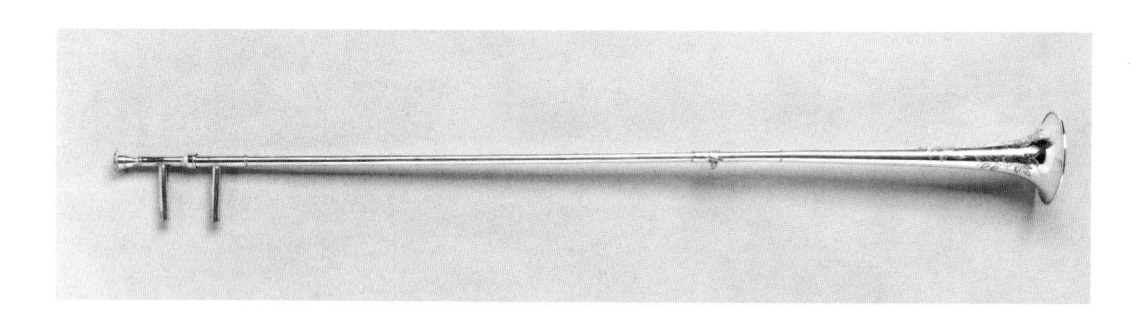

Stringed Instruments

PLUCKED STRING INSTRUMENTS

5.1. MANDORE, probably Italian, *c.*1750–1800

Museum Accession Number 1967.161.43

Unsigned.

Body composed of nine alternating ribs of ebony and ivory. The belly is made from a single piece of pine, carved with a rose in an interlacing, geometric pattern. The ebony fingerboard has seven gut frets and is inlaid with ivory stringing. The nut is also of ivory. The pegbox is of ebony, inlaid with ivory, with an octagonal-shaped finial of alternating ebony and ivory inlay. There are 12 ebony pegs for the six double courses.

Dimensions   Overall length 520mm, length of belly 242mm, width of belly 147mm, string length from nut to bridge 32.5mm, length of neck 120mm.

Provenance   Rushworth and Dreaper Ltd, Liverpool, –1967.

5.2. GUITAR, Johann Friederick Merchel, Stuttgart, 1801

Museum Accession Number 1967.161.31

Label   *Johann Friederick Merchel, Mechanicus & Instrumenten Macher in Stuttgardt, 1801, No.36.*

The belly of a single piece of pine, the flat back and sides of sycamore. The sunken soundhole of carved parchment is set with the initial *B* and decorated around the outer edge with a band of chip-carved decoration. The neck and tapering, turned-back head are of ebony, inlaid with two lighter coloured woods and with ivory along the outer edge. Thirteen ivory frets. Six strings (three gut and three overspun) held by six sycamore pegs. The strings are held on the ebony bridge by six ivory pins, two of them with mother-of-pearl centres. Scrolling moustaches of ebony applied to the belly at either side of the bridge.

Dimensions   Total length, including head 940mm, length of body 450mm, width of bouts 210mm, 180mm, 260mm, depth 92mm, string length 692mm (from top of neck).

Provenance   Rushworth and Dreaper Ltd, Liverpool, 1924–1967.

A note in the archives of Rushworth and Dreaper states that this instrument 'has been in stock over 30 years. Last value (stock) 1924 – £1.5.0'.

References   R & D catalogue 1 (undated), not paginated.
R & D catalogue 2 (undated), p.9.
Bevan, 1990, p.68.

Guitar, detail.

Guitar

5.3. MANDOLIN, Carlo Albertini and Sons, Milan, early twentieth century

Museum Accession Number 1967.161.37

Label now missing (?)

Body composed of 15 alternating ribs of stained sycamore. The belly is made from a single piece of pine, with a kidney-shaped sound-hole, decorated around the edge with ebony inlaid with mother-of-pearl. The outer edge of the belly is decorated in a similar manner, with inlaid mother-of-pearl. The protective plate below the sound-hole is of ebony. The fingerboard, with 18 metal frets, is of a dark wood, possibly rosewood, and extends onto the belly. The edge of the pegbox is decorated with an inlaid light coloured wood in a feathered pattern. The curled, flattened square head is decorated with applied mother-of-pearl. The six pegs are arranged vertically to the pegbox, with brass mounts and heads of bone. The six single strings are of gut and overspun metal. Ebony bridge with inlaid mother-of-pearl flowerheads.

Dimensions	Overall length 546mm, length of belly 300mm, width of belly 220mm, string length from nut to bridge 325mm.
Maker	Carlo Albertini (1866–1940).
Provenance	Rushworth and Dreaper Ltd, Liverpool, –1967.
	Although the original label appears to be missing, a record in Rushworth and Dreaper's archives gives the name of the maker as 'Carlo Albertinie Figlio', and notes that it had 'been in stock many years. Value about £2'.
References	R & D catalogue 1 (undated), not paginated. R & D catalogue 2 (undated), p.9. Bevan, 1990, p.68.

5.4. BANJO, unsigned, *c.*1850–1910

Museum Accession Number 1987.213

Unsigned.

This instrument is made from two separate banjos married together. The neck and head, of mahogany inlaid with mother-of-pearl motifs and two yellow glass pastes, is from a hand-made minstrel banjo of the mid nineteenth century. The hoop, of ash and brass, is from a factory-made banjo of the late nineteenth or early twentieth century, *c.*1870–1910.

Vellum-covered head. Replacement ebony nut. The instrument originally had seven strings, including the drone string for the thumb. It was later altered to six strings, leaving the original nut with 11 string notches. The nut was then inverted and cut again for six strings, resulting in very unevenly spaced notches and causing some splitting to the head. Due to this the original nut has been removed (1993) and a properly fitting replacement nut attached. Seven replacement strings, three gut and four overspun, have been added (1993), and are held by six celluloid pegs in the head and one celluloid thumb-peg.

The mahogany dowel-stick has been re-cut at some point with a hand-saw, leaving irregular steps in it. The neck is attached to the hoop by means of a wedge-plate on the dowel-stick. This is a modern replacement (1993) since the existing wedge-plate was a badly fitted earlier addition. The dowel-stick has been shortened at some point, and a piece of wood added to it to accommodate the end pin screw. The hoop originally had 12 brass brackets. A further 32 have been added at some later date. A modern bridge of beech has been added (1993) and a better fitting bracket hook and nut on the tailpiece.

Dimensions   Total length 877mm, width of hoop 300mm, depth 65mm, length of neck including head 575mm, string length from nut 715mm.

Provenance   Presented by Mr Eric Richards, 1987.

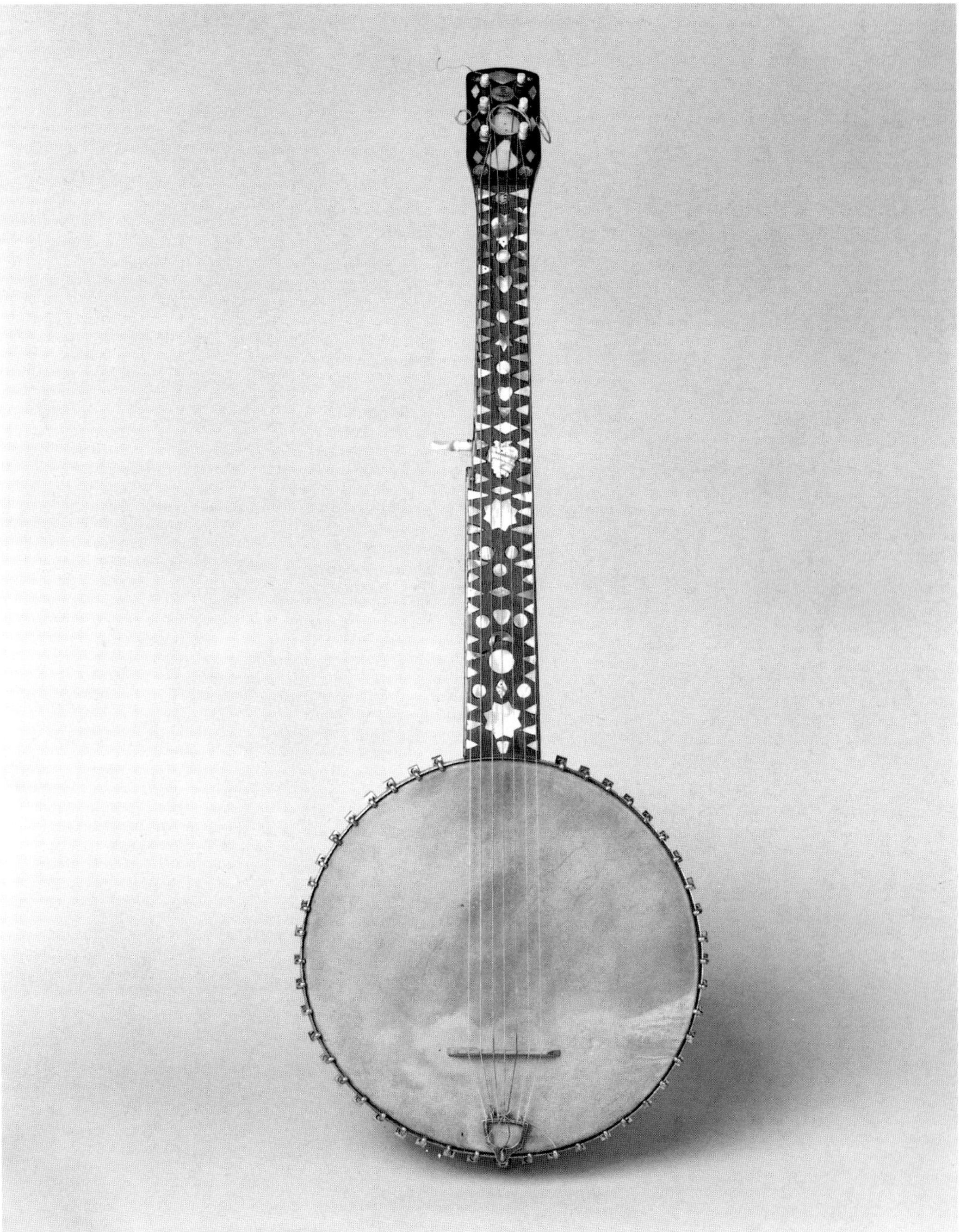

5.5. BALALAIKA, Russian, late nineteenth–early twentieth century

Museum Accession Number 58.111.1

No label visible.

Body composed of seven ribs of sycamore divided by ebony stringing. The belly is made from a single piece of pine, edged with ebony and inlaid with a light wood stringing. The head and neck are of sycamore, the head and fingerboard veneered with ebony. Nineteen metal frets on the fingerboard, and four inlaid motifs of bone and mother-of-pearl. The bridge is of beech. Three steel strings, held by three steel wrest pins and tuned by bone pegs. Engraved steel plate on the back of the head, worked with stylised floral motif. Front of the head set with a silver Russian coin, a four-kopeck piece. Four small square sound-holes, forming the windows of the house-shaped ebony veneer on the belly.

Dimensions   Overall length 695mm, width 415mm, depth 120mm.

Provenance   Presented by Mrs E. Wilson, 1958.

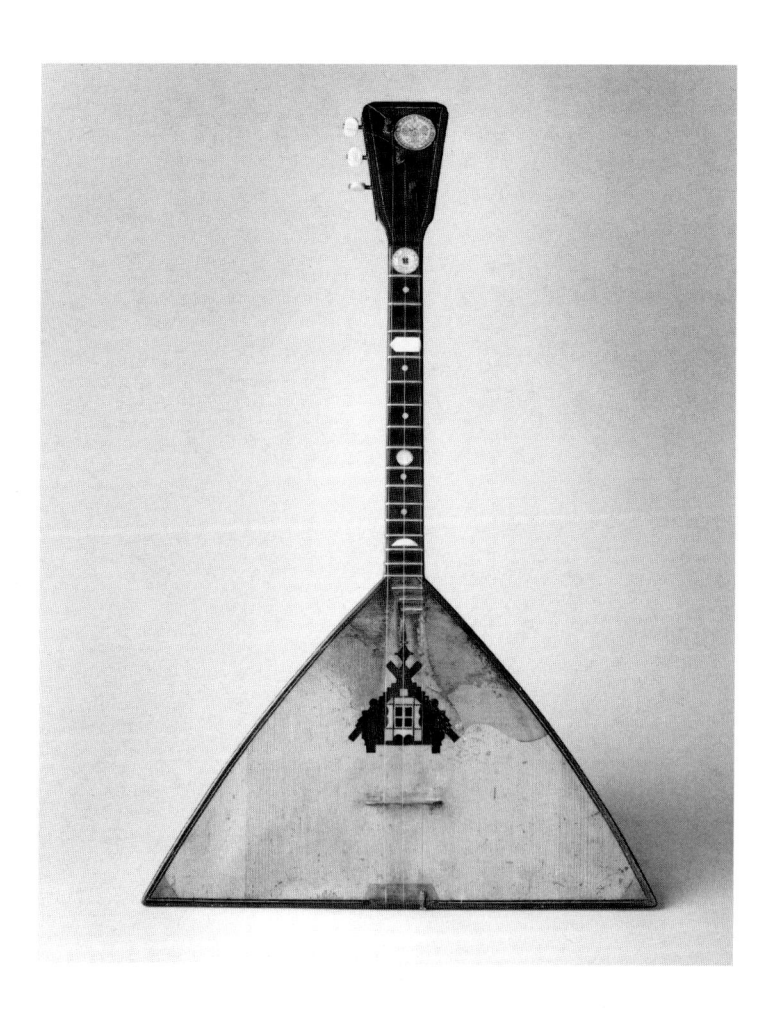

5.6. BALALAIKA, Russian, *c.*1900–1920

Museum Accession Number 58.111.2

Label *Torgovy dom, Bratya Grimm, S.P.B. Nevsky Pr. No.102* on metal plate on back of head, and has piece of newspaper (?) stuck inside soundhole, possibly from repair, printed *Russki Dramaticheski Teatr.*

Body and base composed of seven ribs of sycamore divided with ebony stringing. The belly is made from a single piece of pine, edged with ebony and inlaid with a light wood stringing. Ebonised neck and head and fingerboard of ebony, with 23 steel frets, inlaid with five mother-of-pearl motifs. Applied, shaped 'plate' of walnut, extending from base of neck to below sound-hole, with border of ivory stringing. Two corners and centre base of belly also veneered with walnut, edged with ivory stringing. The surround of the circular sound-hole is veneered with beech and inlaid with ebony and ivory stringing.

The bridge is of beech. Three modern replacement gut strings, tuned by four metal pegs with bone ends. Head inlaid with oval-shaped amber bead. In own canvas case.

Dimensions Overall length 685mm, width 405mm, depth 110mm.

Provenance Presented by Mrs E. Wilson, 1958.

5.7. BASS BALALAIKA, Russian, *c.*1920–1940

Museum Accession Number 1977.291

Inscription *Modeli U. Ziuzina* on metal plate on back of head.

Label *Masterska Musikalnikh Instrumentov Ivana Abromovicha Ziuzina* inside soundhole.

Body and base composed of seven ribs of birch. The belly is made from a single piece of pine, edged with ebony and inlaid with a light wood stringing. Neck and head of birch. The fingerboard is of ebony, with 14 metal frets and five inlaid mother-of-pearl fret markers. The bridge is of beech. Four strings, three of overspun copper, one modern overspun replacement, tuned by steel wrest pins and bone pegs. The circular sound-hole is decorated around the outer edge with veneer of beech and ebony and lighter wood stringing. Applied ebony 'plate' below the sound-hole.

Applied steel plate on back of head, engraved with stylised, scrolling decoration. Adjustable steel spike in right hand corner of body. In own canvas case.

Dimensions Overall length 1370mm, width 910mm, depth 260mm.

Provenance Presented by Mr H. Braden, 1977.

This instrument was given to the donor in 1970 by Mr Tarrant Bailey Jnr.

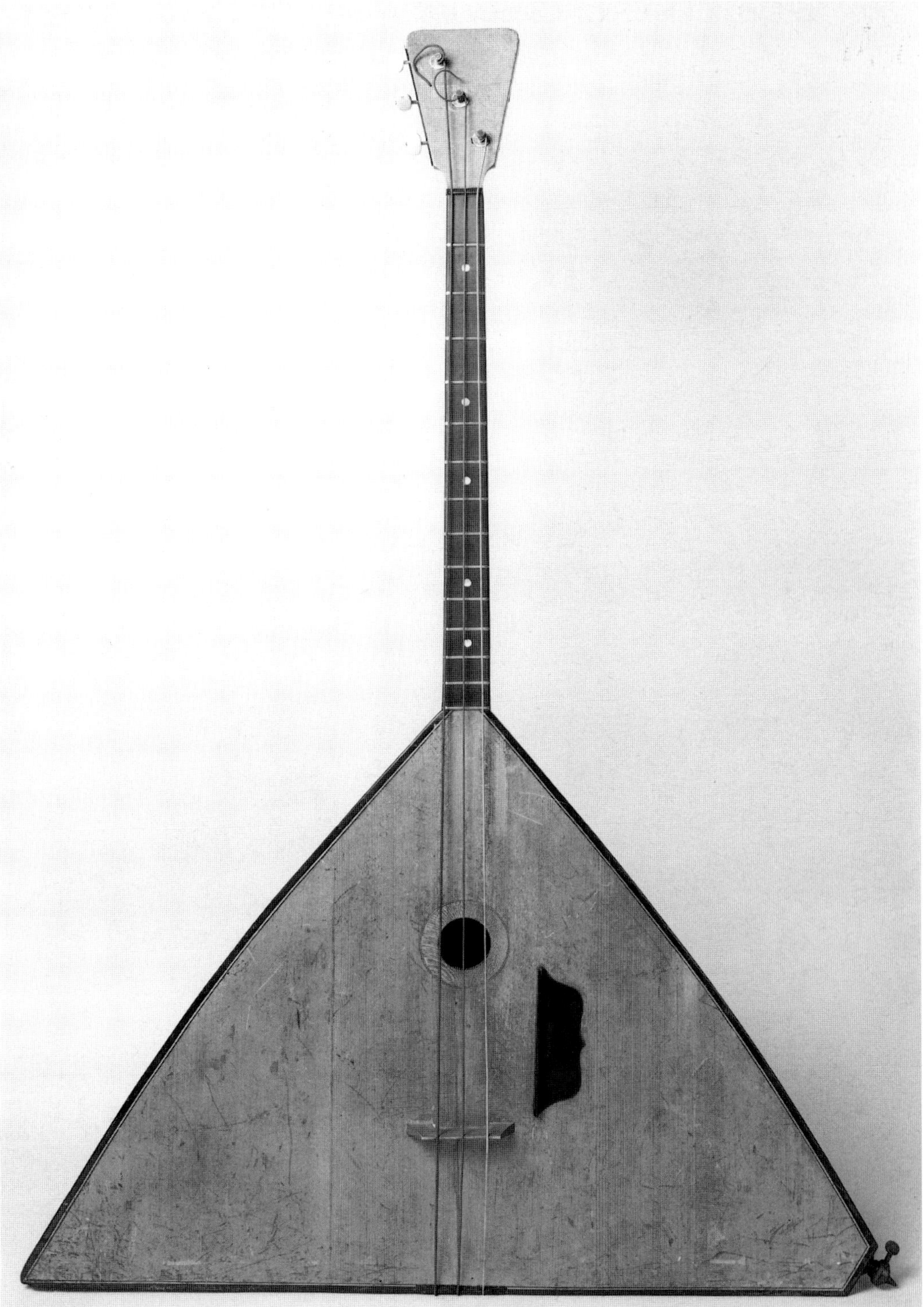

5.8. APOLLO LYRE, Clementi and Co., London, *c.*1810

Museum Accession Number 1967.161.46

Inscription	*Clementi & Co., London* in gold paint on belly, below fingerboard.
	Lyre-shaped, with central neck like that of a guitar. Back of sycamore, in two pieces, the sides also of sycamore decorated with painted gold 'stringing' around the edges. The belly is a single piece of varnished pine, painted around the edges with scrolling gold acanthus leaves, urns and griffins' heads on a painted black ground. The sound-hole is filled with a gilt star-shaped rose and is painted around the outer edge with a gold border of scrolling leaves on a black ground. Bridge of ebony with an ivory slip, the belly decorated above and below the bridge with painted gold musical trophies. Ebonised neck and head, ebony fingerboard, ivory nut and 15 ivory frets. Six strings, three gut and three overspun, held by six steel wrestpins in the back of the head. The 'arms' of the instrument, ending in acorn-shaped finials, have been painted with modern gold paint at some point. Stands on an ebonised and gilt rectangular plinth with applied gilt balls around the edges.
Dimensions	Height 835mm, length of belly, excluding 'arms', 360mm, width 363mm, depth 105mm, string length from nut 572mm.
Provenance	Rushworth and Dreaper Ltd, Liverpool, –1967.
References	R & D catalogue 2 (undated), p.2. Bevan, 1990, p.68.

5.9. DITAL HARP, Edward Light, London, *c.*1818

Museum Accession Number 1967.161.44

Inscription	*Ed. Light, Gt. Marylebone Street, London, Patent Dital Harp, No.39* in gold paint on flat top of body.
	Body of pine, painted dark blue-black and decorated all over with gold paint. Edge of belly decorated with scrolling gold vine leaves, stylised floral spray and fake sound-hole and surround, with star-shaped rose. The pin-bridge, with ivory-inlaid edge, is positioned diagonally across the body. The neck, or 'harmonic curve', is supported by a carved, fluted column, decorated with gold paint. Nineteen gut strings (one missing), held at the back of the neck with steel wrestpins. Fourteen of the strings have 'ditals', flat-headed buttons, each with its note painted beside it in gold paint. The dital devices, when depressed by the thumb, grip the strings and raise their pitch by a semi-tone. Small fingerboard with 13 bone frets for the other five strings. Two oval-shaped sound-holes in the back. Oval-shaped base with moulded gilt composition border.
Dimensions	Height 887mm, width 365mm, string lengths 305mm–760mm.
Maker	Edward Light (*c.*1747–*c.*1832) invented and manufactured a number of novelty stringed instruments, including the harp-guitar, the harp-lute and the harp-lyre. He appears to have patented his design for a dital harp in 1816.
Provenance	Rushworth and Dreaper Ltd, Liverpool, 1953–1967.
	Rushworth and Dreaper purchased this instrument from a Mrs Broadsmith of Lancashire on 30th July, 1953 for the sum of £3.3.0.
References	R & D catalogue 2 (undated), p.10.

5.10. PEDAL HARP, J. Erat and Sons, London, c.1800–1810

Museum Accession Number 56.208

Inscription *J. Erat & Sons, Wardour Street, Soho, London, 1235* along the neck.

Round-backed soundbox of black laquered wood, with five rectangular flaps in the central section, decorated with 'Grecian'-style figures and musical trophies in gold paint. Black laquered and fluted column, terminating in gilt gesso capital 'supported' by three winged female caryatids, and decorated with bands of palmettes and with a band of mermaids bearing lyres and trumpets. Front of pedalbox, on four simple paw feet, and base of column also covered in gilt gesso, decorated with stylised scrolling foliage and lyres, with two applied lions on upper part of the pedalbox, either side of column. Back of pedalbox decorated with alternating vertical stripes of gold and orange paint. Single row of 'fourchettes' along the neck, operated by seven single-lever type brass pedals, with coil springs in pedalbox. An eighth pedal operates the flaps in the back of the soundbox. Upper surface of neck painted with a repeating pattern of grapes and vines. Soundboard painted with two pairs of stylised 'Grecian' figures playing instruments, and with two musical trophies in gold, set within a broad, painted border of foliage, figures and grotesques.

Compass 43 strings, EE – c^3.

Dimensions Height 1680mm, maximum string length 1485mm.

Maker According to the local trade directories, Jacob Erat, harpmaker, was based at 100 Wardour Street, London, between 1802 and 1817. In 1818, the entries begin to refer to him as John Erat, but he remained at the same address until 1822 when he appears to have acquired additional premises at 23 Berner Street. Between 1833 and *c.*1858, Jacob and James Erat were based solely at 23 Berner Street. After 1859, the premises were taken over by another firm and the Erats disappear from the directories.

Provenance Presented by Mr T.E. Williams, 1956.

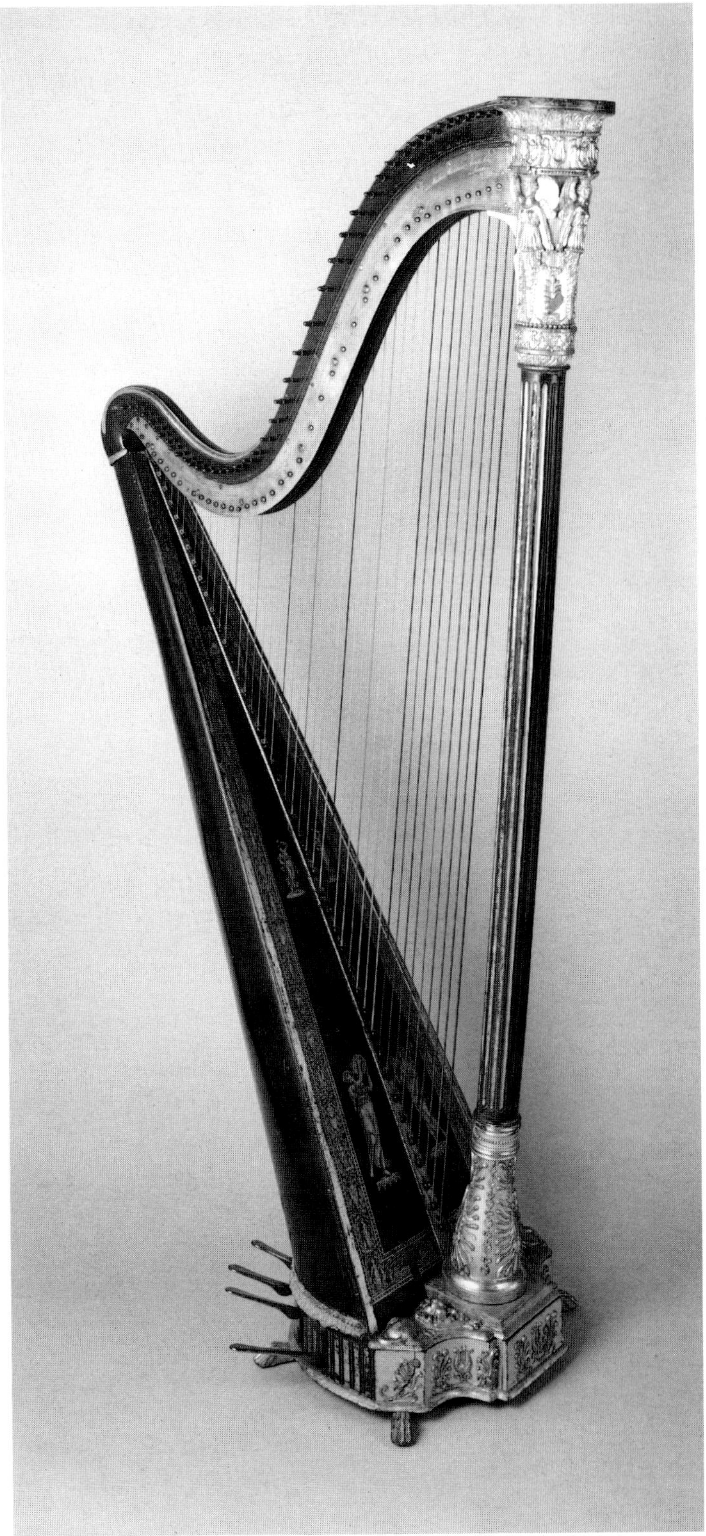

5.11. PEDAL HARP, J. and J. Erat, London, *c.*1836–1837

Museum Accession Number 1970.166

Inscription *J & J Erat, Patent Harp Manufacturers, 23 Berners Street, London, No. 2343* with the coat of arms of William IV, along the neck.

Round-backed soundbox veneered with satinwood, with decorative varnished finish, edged on both sides with beech. Five rectangular holes in the soundbox, their original flaps and the pedal which operated them now missing. Cylindrical column decorated with applied gilt beading in the Gothic style, and terminating in a six-sided gilt gesso-covered capital. Five of the facets decorated with applied figures, playing cymbals and tambourines beneath canopies of Gothic tracery. Pierced Gothic canopy all around top of capital, largely a modern replacement (1993) for display purposes. Neck, decorated with painted gold foliage, coach lines and gold beading, springs from sixth facet of capital. Two rows of linked 'fourchettes' along the neck, operated by seven brass pedals. Front and top of pedalbox, supported on four scrolling feet, and base of column all covered with gilt gesso and decorated with applied, scrolling foliage and Gothic architectural motifs. Back of pedalbox decorated with border of gilt gesso acanthus leaves on a punched, gilt gesso ground. Front of pedalbox a modern reconstruction (1993) for display purposes. Plain pine soundboard and beech bridge both later replacements. With matching leather-covered swivel chair, painted music stand, circular string box and rectangular tool box.

Compass	44 strings, EE – f³.
Dimensions	Height 1710mm, maximum string length 1475mm.
Provenance	Bequest of Mrs F.V. Gore-Langton, 1970.

5.12. ZITHER ('Saltzburg' zither), German or Austrian, c.1860–1870

Museum Accession Number WAG 1993.86

Unsigned.

'Saltzburg'-form zither, the body of pine veneered with rosewood, the top edges decorated with ivory stringing, the sides inlaid with a light wood stringing. Base and bottom lip of ebonised pine. Fingerboard of ebony with 30 metal frets and eight inlaid mother-of-pearl fret markers. Five melody strings on the fingerboard, three steel and two overspun, held by five pegs with ivory heads, and 27 accompanying strings, held by steel wrestpins. Brass plate at top left hand corner, engraved with a swan, scrolling vine leaves and stylised flowerheads. Sound-hole surround inlaid with mother-of-pearl on an ebonised ground, edged with ivory stringing and border. Three turned ivory feet on base.

Dimensions Length 500mm, width 310mm.

Provenance Unknown.

5.13. ZITHER, Menzenhauer, U.S.A., *c*.1895–1900

Museum Accession Number 1973.71

Transfer print — *Menzenhauer's Guitar Zither, Patented May 29th, 1894* on the case.

Body of ebonised pine. Sound-hole decorated with coloured transfer-printed design around outer edge. Scale, across width of body, also a coloured transfer print. Thirty-one steel strings, modern replacements (1993), held by steel wrestpins. Three brass ball feet on the base.

Dimensions — Length 475mm, width 32.3mm.

Provenance — Presented by Mr L. Cartwright, 1973.

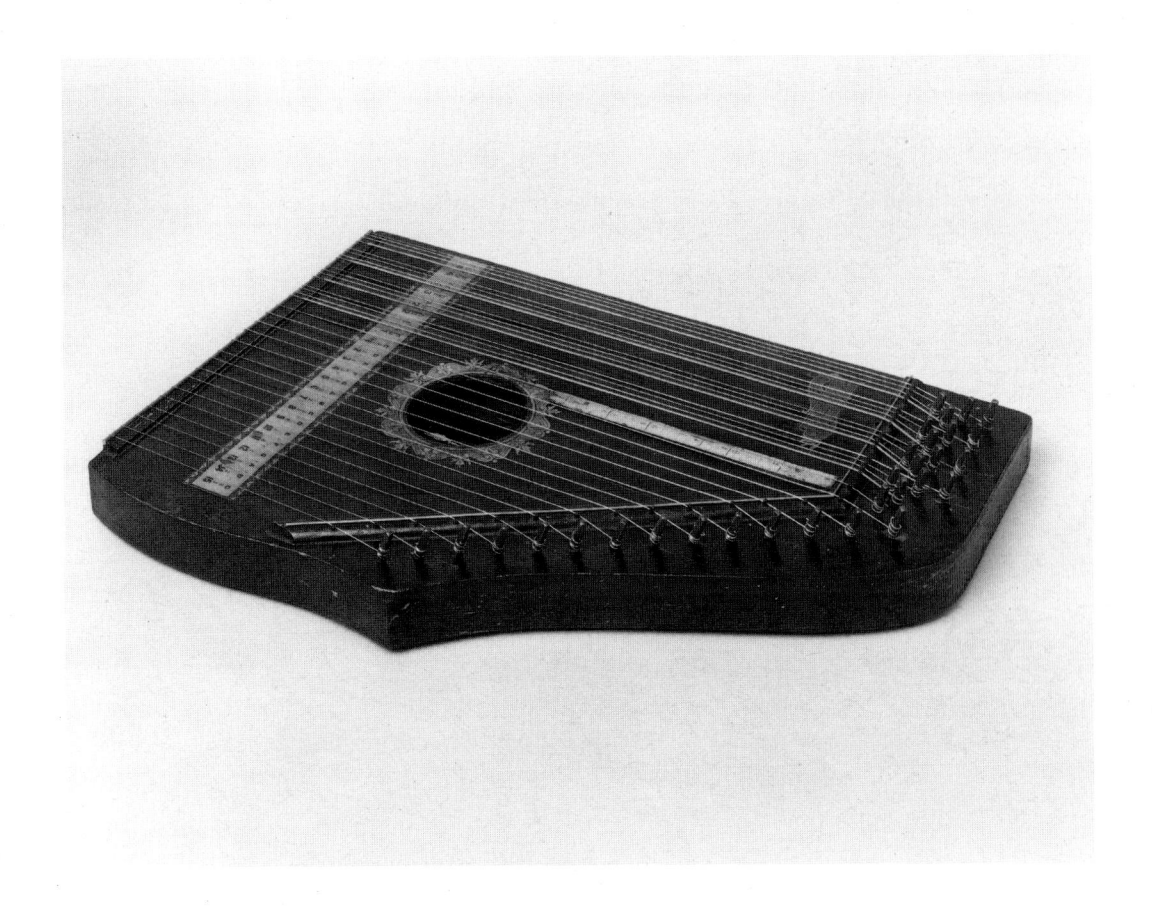

5.14. ZITHER, the Anglo-American Zither Company, c.1899–1910

Museum Accession Number 1964.300

Label *Lion Zither, Patented, Manufactured by the* (illegible) *Zither Co., New York, London, Melbourne. Sold through our special agents only.*

Transfer Print *Lion Zither, Patented October 7th 1899, The Anglo-American Zither Co., New York, London, Melbourne* on the case.

Body of ebonised pine. Decorated with coloured, transfer-printed scrolled design around the edges of the case top and the border of the sound-hole. Two coloured, transfer-printed scales applied to the case. Two sets of strings, crossing each other diagonally, the majority of them modern steel and overspun replacements (1993), all held by 47 steel wrestpins. Three conical brass feet on base. In own wooden case.

Dimensions Length 506mm, width 365mm.

Provenance Purchased from F. Akin, 1964.

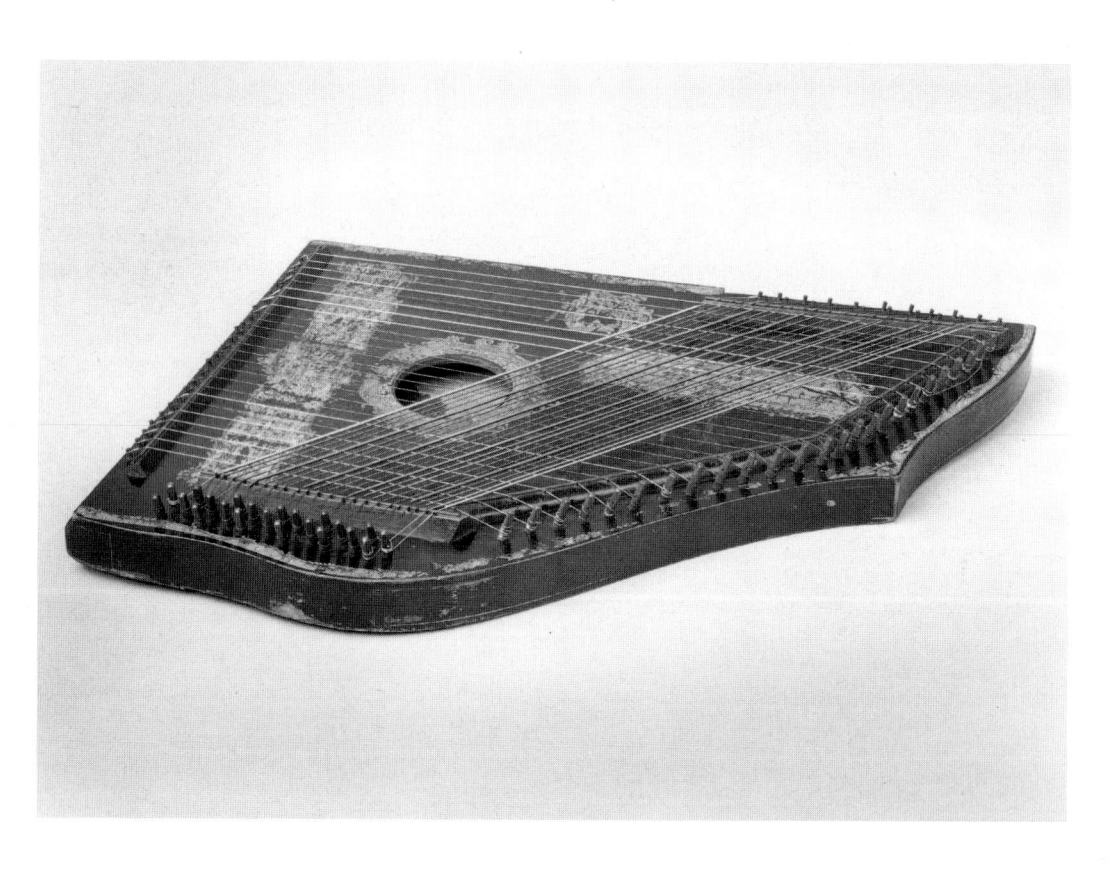

5.15. ZITHER (Autoharp Zither), T. Meinhold, Saxony, c.1900

Museum Accession Number WAG 1993.87

Label *Made in Saxony, T. Meinhold's Autoharp, Accord-Zither-Harfe, Gebrauchsmuster No. 4827* in printed celluloid on the case, and *T. Meinhold, Made in Germany, Patent, Vollkommenstes Instrument der Gegenwar*t on paper inside the soundboard.

Stamp *Made in Germany*

Body of ebonised pine, veneered with rosewood on the case front. Bridge of ebonised pine. Case decorated with coloured transfer print of wild flowers. Scale printed on strip of celluloid applied to lower half of case. Thirty-seven strings, some of them modern replacements (1993), held by steel wrestpins. Thirteen chord dampers over the strings, held in a frame of ebonised pine. Five brass ball feet on the base. In own wooden case.

Dimensions Length 540mm, width 337mm.

Provenance Unknown.

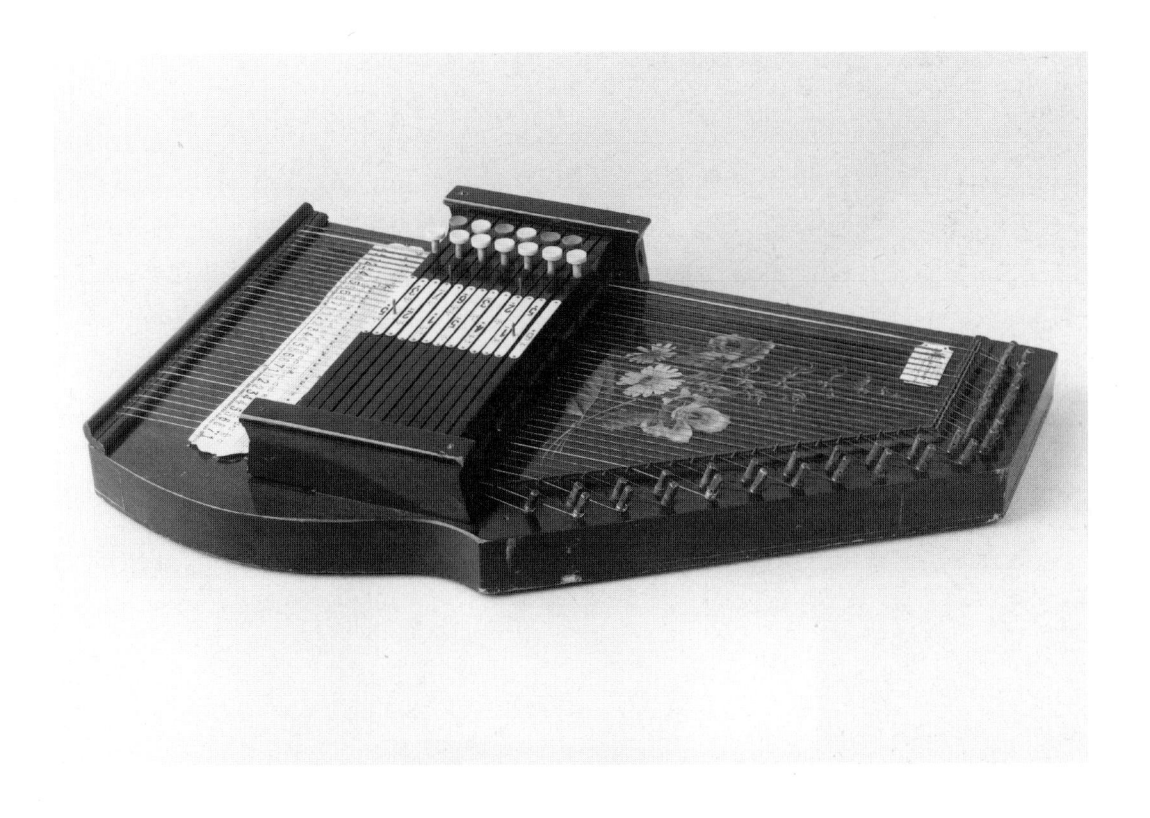

5.16. DULCIMER, unsigned, probably eastern European, mid-late nineteenth century

Museum Accession Number 1969.201.2

Unsigned.

Trapezium-shaped soundbox with hinged lid. Lid, frame, wrestplank and hitchplank all of mahogany. Two replacement bridges of black-stained mahogany topped with brass wire, each with seven circles cut into them, carrying 17 triple courses of replacement wire strings (1993). Soundboard of cedar with two gilt-paper roses in the form of stylised flowerheads. Four rectangular wooden feet on the base.

Dimensions Length at front 795mm, length at back 430mm, height 95mm, depth, including case, 400mm.

Provenance Presented by Mrs Batterson, 1969.

5.17. DULCIMER, unsigned, probably eastern European, late 19th century

Museum Accession Number 48.35

Unsigned.

Large trapezium-shaped soundbox of stained pine, the sides veneered with rectangular panels of mahogany. Both bridges and all the strings now missing. Wrestplank and hitchplank of beech, the original steel wrestpins still present. Two intricately carved parchment roses in the main soundboard section and another in the smaller soundboard section on the right-hand side. Both soundboards now split in several places. Two wooden brackets on base, possibly for attachment to a stand. This instrument is in very poor condition.

Dimensions Total length 1290mm, width 370mm, depth 70mm.

Provenance Presented by Mr K.C. Jackson, 1948.

5.18. GUSLI, unsigned, Russian, *c*.1900–1920

Museum Accession Number 58.111.3

Unsigned.

Irregular, trapezoid-shaped body. Soundboard and two of the sides of pine, the two shorter sides of beech. Base of ebonised pine. Hitchplank and bridge both of beech. Thirteen strings, 12 of steel and one overspun, held by steel wrestpins. Plain, circular sound-hole with mid nineteenth century 50–kopeck note stuck inside it. Small motif of ebony and ivory applied to the soundboard.

Dimensions Length of sides 525mm, 380mm, 290mm, 110mm.

Provenance Presented by Mrs E. Wilson, 1958.

BOWED STRING INSTRUMENTS

5.19. KIT (?), unsigned, *c.*1750–1800

Museum Accession Number 1967.161.35

Label	*Restored by John Corsby, South Quarter, Northampton.*
	Belly of a single piece of pine, with two f-shaped soundholes, the back of a single piece of sycamore and the sides of sycamore. Neck and scrolled head of sycamore. Fingerboard, nut and tailpiece of ebony. Bridge of beech. Four gut strings held by sycamore pegs in the head.
Dimensions	Total length 475mm, width of bouts 110mm, 80mm, 125mm, depth 26mm, string length to nut 332mm.
Maker	The original maker of this instrument is unknown, but its repairer, John Corsby, musical instrument maker, is recorded in the town's poll books as working in Bridge Street, Northampton during the 1790s. According to the rate books for his parish, All Saints', Northampton, he appears to have first begun work in Bridge Street in 1787 and remained there until 1813.
Provenance	Rushworth and Dreaper Ltd, Liverpool, 1918–1967.
	Rushworth and Dreaper purchased this instrument from (the dealers ?) Ball Beavan of London in 1918 for the sum of £1.10.0. Although they referred to it as a kit, its proportions may suggest that it was made as a miniature or child's violin.
References	R & D catalogue 1 (undated), not paginated. R & D catalogue 2 (undated), p.8, p.9, (two editions). Whittington-Egan, 1976, p.158. Bevan, 1990, p.68.

5.20. VIOLA D'AMORE (converted to a Quinton), Johann Ulrich Eberle, Prague, 1759

Museum Accession Number 1967.161.33

Label	*Johannes Udalricus Eberle fecit, Prague, 1759.*
	Belly of a single piece of pine, with two flame-shaped soundholes. The back of two pieces of sycamore joined with a narrow strip of ebony down the centre. Sides, neck and scrolled head of sycamore. Fingerboard, nut and tailpiece all of ebony. Small, intricately carved rose below the fingerboard, with narrow, inlaid border of ebony. Five strings, two gut, three overspun, held by five ebony pegs in the head. The neck, fingerboard and tailpiece are all of a later date, added presumably when the instrument was converted to its present five-stringed form, possibly during the late eighteenth century.
Dimensions	Total length 680mm, width of bouts 190mm, 140mm, 230mm, depth 60mm, string length from nut to tailpiece 480mm.
Maker	Johann Ulrich Eberle (1699–1768) specialised in the making of violins and violas d'amore.
Provenance	Rushworth and Dreaper Ltd, Liverpool, 1922–1967.
	Rushworth and Dreaper purchased this instrument in Markneukirchen, Germany, from Peter Harlau, through (the dealer ?) George Krenke, for the sum of £5.0.0.
References	R & D catalogue 1 (undated), not paginated.
	R & D catalogue 2 (undated), p.8.

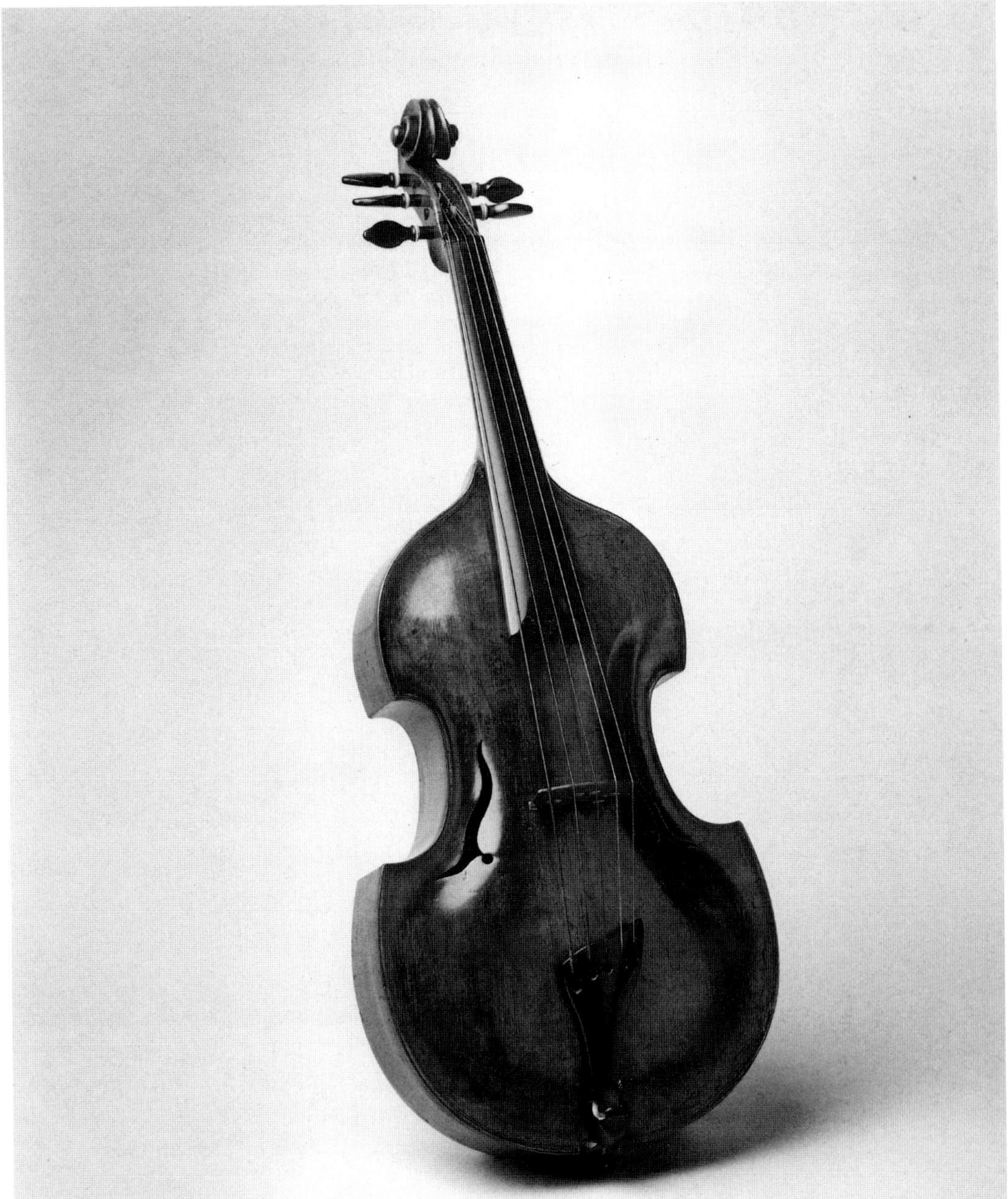

5.21. VIOLONCELLO, James and Henry Banks, Liverpool, *c*.1820

Museum Accession Number WAG 1991.77

Stamp *J & H Banks, Liverpool* on the back.

Belly of a single piece of pine, the back of two pieces of sycamore, the sides of sycamore. Inlaid purfling on back and front of two black lines and one light line. Neck and scrolled head of sycamore. Fingerboard, nut and tailpiece of ebony, modern replacement bridge of beech. Two f-shaped soundholes in belly. Four modern overspun strings, held by four sycamore pegs. Modern steel spike. In own fitted wooden case.

Dimensions Total length 1195mm, length of belly 710mm, width of bouts 315mm, 230mm, 370mm, depth 123mm, string length from tailpiece to nut 775mm.

Maker The Banks brothers, James and Henry, started up in business in Church Street, Liverpool, in 1811. They remained there until 1830, when they moved to Bold Street, but by 1831 both brothers had died.

Provenance Purchased, private treaty sale, via Sotheby's. Failed to sell, Sotheby's, 14th March, 1991, lot 91.

References Sale catalogue, Sotheby's, 14th March, 1991, pp.58–59, lot 91.

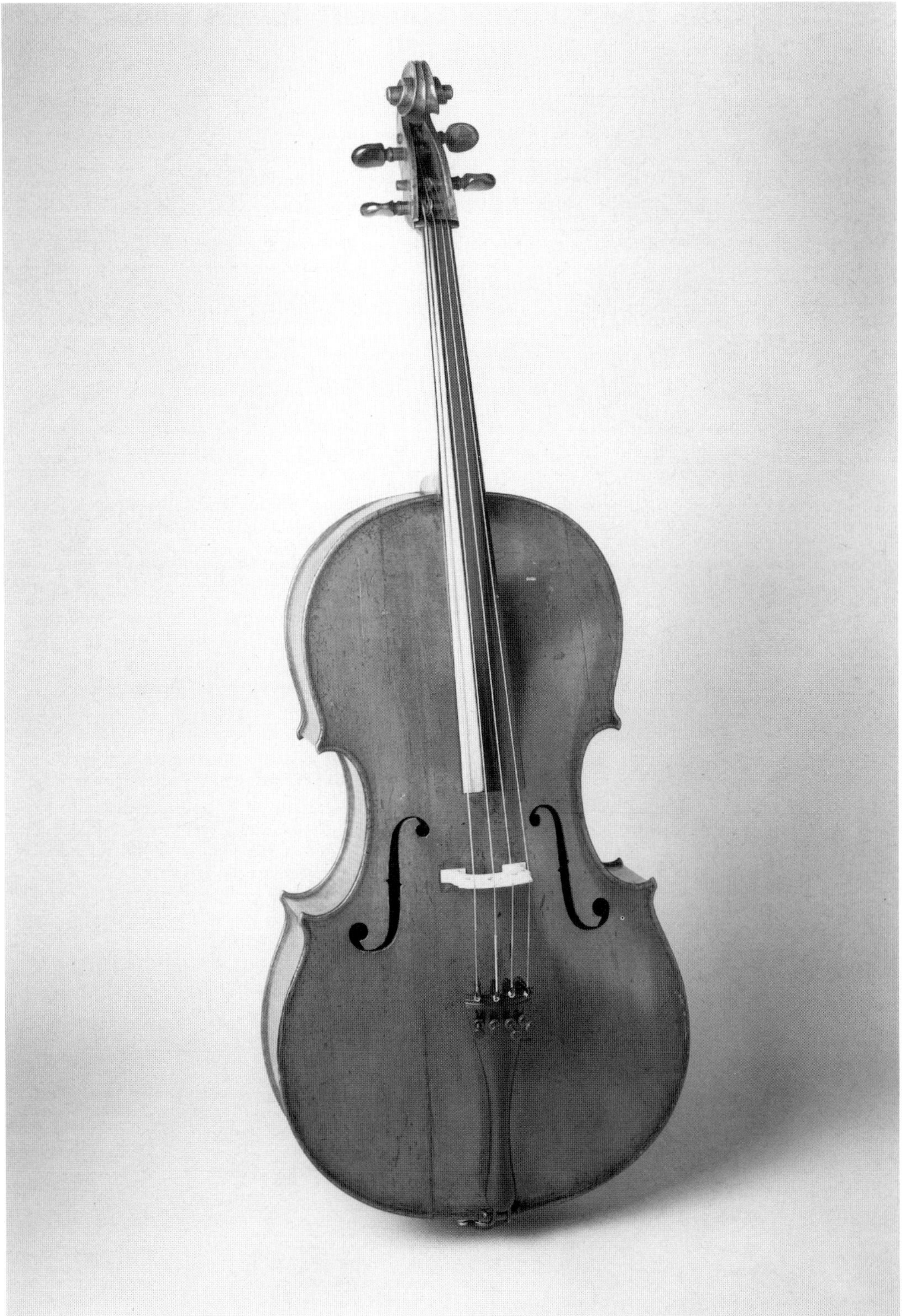

5.22. DOUBLE BASS, Edward Stansfield, Liverpool, 1927

Museum Accession Number 57.58

Stamp *Stansfield, Liverpool* on the metal plate on the head, and *E. Stansfield, Liverpool, 1927* on the bridge.

Inscription *This bass made for Sir Hamilton Harty and the Halle Orchestra by Edward Stansfield, 1927*, on oval silver plate mounted on ebony, on the back, and *To my dear friend, James Parkinson Esq, I dedicate this instrument, E. Stansfield, 15 Granby St, Liverpool, 1927, No.1*, inside the back in ink, with *Make a nice noise and a loud one, Eliz. H. Stansfield*, and *Just to wish the best of luck, Stella*, both in pencil. Also, inscribed in ink on a label, *Good luck and an honourable life to this double bass, Hamilton Harty, March 1927*, across seven bars of the double bass part from Beethoven's Fifth Symphony. In pencil inside the belly *Made by E. Stansfield, 15 Granby St, Liverpool, 1927, an experimental 5 string bass, began Nov. 5th 1926, closed up March 9th 1927.*

Belly of a single piece of pine, with two large f-shaped soundholes, the back of 10 pieces of sycamore with narrow band of ebony running across the width. Sides of sycamore, inlaid with two strips of ebony on each side. Back and front inlaid with purfling of two dark lines and one light line. Neck and scrolled head of sycamore. Fingerboard, mouldings at back of neck and nut all of ebony. Tailpiece of mahogany inlaid with two narrow decorative bands of stained green wood, ebony and boxwood, and with oval cartouche of urn and flowers, also in stained green wood and boxwood. Bridge of beech. Five strings (three gut, two overspun, one of these a modern replacement), held in the chrome-plated head by five chromed pegs with screw adjustments.

Dimensions Total length 2045mm, length of belly 1200mm, width of bouts 575mm, 407mm, 677mm, depth 270mm, string length from bridge to tailpiece 1330mm.

Maker Edward Stansfield (1873–1940) was a double bass player of some repute with both the Halle Orchestra and the Liverpool Philharmonic Orchestra. Sir Herbert Hamilton Harty (1880–1941) was a well-known composer-conductor who also worked with the Halle and Liverpool Philharmonic Orchestras.

Provenance Presented by the Royal Liverpool Philharmonic Society, 1957.

References Liverpool Echo, March 24, 1927, p.4.

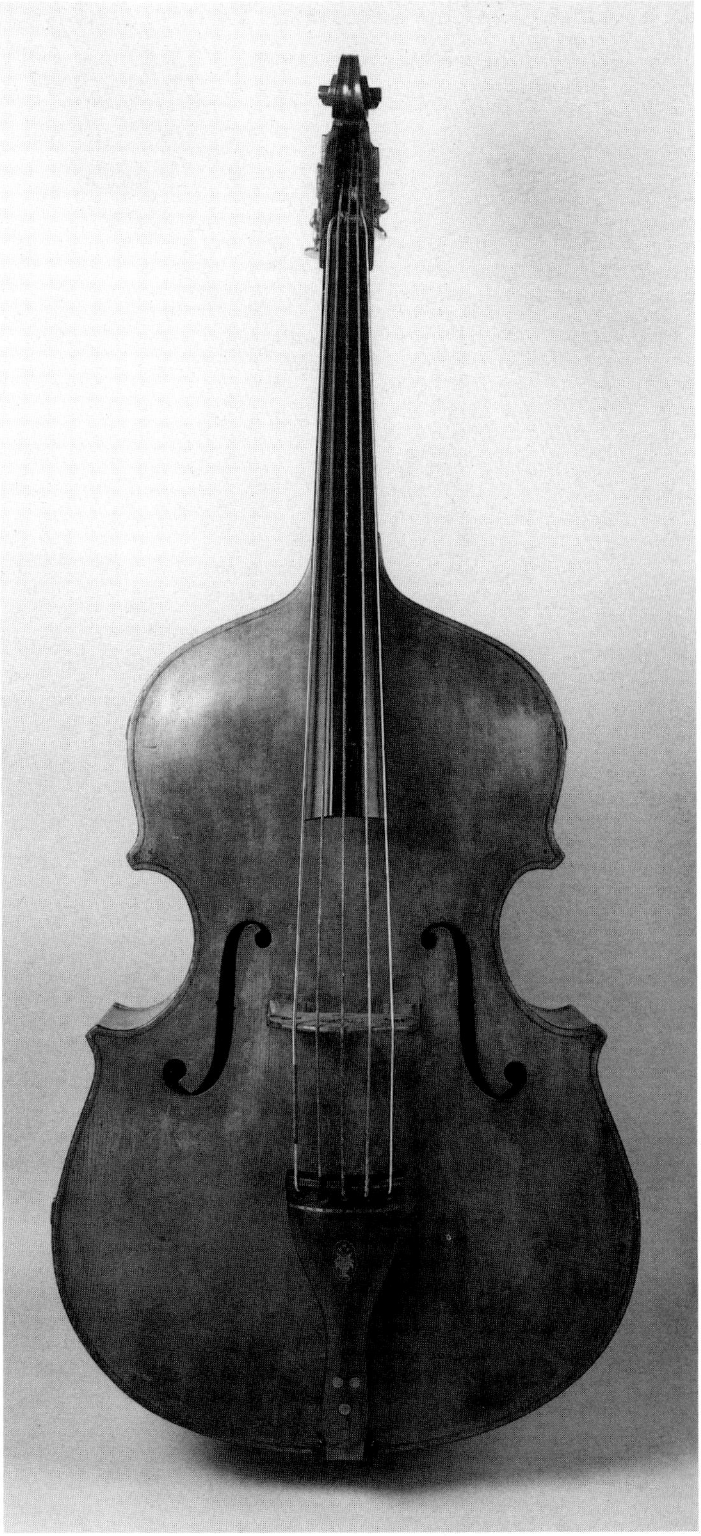

5.23. CITHER VIOL, Thomas Perry and William Wilkinson, Dublin, 1792

Museum Accession Number 1967.161.32

Label	*Made by Thos. Perry and Wm. Wilkinson, Musical Instrument Makers, No.6 Anglesea Street, Dublin, 1792, No.1863.*
Stamp	*No.1863, Perry, Dublin* on back.
	Belly of a single piece of pine, with two flame-shaped soundholes. The back of a single piece of sycamore. Sides, neck and long, tapering head all of sycamore, the square-shaped finial set with ebony, mother-of-pearl and a stained green wood in the form of a star. Fingerboard, nut and tailpiece of ivory, the tailpiece set with a small silver plate and ivory pins. Bridge of beech. Four double courses of metal strings and two single overspun strings, held by ring-shaped brass pegs on brass and ivory mounts, and brass gears enclosed in the head.
Dimensions	Total length 740mm, width of bouts 185mm, 130mm, 200mm, depth 44mm, string length from nut to tailpiece 400mm.
Makers	Thomas Perry (1744 ? 1757 ?–1818), is best known for his violins. He included the name of his son-in-law, William Wilkinson, on his labels from about 1787 onwards, but Wilkinson does not appear to have taken an active part in the business until after his father-in-law's death in 1818. Thereafter, he continued to use the label with both names on his own violins until about 1839.
Provenance	Charles van Raalte, Brownsea Island, Dorset, –1925. Sir Arthur Wheeler, Brownsea Island, Dorset, 1925–1927. Rushworth and Dreaper Ltd, Liverpool, 1927–1967. Rushworth and Dreaper purchased this instrument from Sir Arthur Wheeler of Brownsea Castle, Brownsea Island, on 21st June, 1927 for the sum of £4.10.0.
References	Sale catalogue, Fox and Sons, 1927, p.109, lot 1784.

5.24. VIOLIN, Rushworth and Dreaper, Liverpool, c.1920s

Museum Accession Number 1988.181

Label   *The 'Artist Apollo', Trade Mark, Rushworth and Dreaper, Liverpool, Style 12, No.1928.*

Belly of a single piece of pine, with two f-shaped soundholes, the back of two pieces of sycamore. Back and front inlaid with purfling of two dark lines and one light line. Sides, neck and scrolled head all of sycamore. Fingerboard, nut, tailpiece and scored chinrest all of ebony. Bridge of beech. Four strings (one steel, two gut, one overspun), held in the head by ebony pegs. With bow, in own fitted case of brown crocodile skin, lined with red velvet and labelled inside, *Rushworth and Dreaper Ltd, Orchestral Instrument Specialists, 11–17 Islington, Liverpool.*

Dimensions   Total length 600mm, width of bouts 163mm, 120mm, 190mm, depth 40mm, string length from nut to tailpiece 390mm.

Provenance   Purchased from Sotheby's, 31st March, 1988, lot 260.

References   Sale catalogue, Sotheby's, 31st March, 1988, p.184, lot 260.

5.25. 'JAPANESE FIDDLE', unsigned, *c.*1900–1920

Museum Accession Number 58.111.4

Unsigned.

Belly made from a single piece of pine, with two f-shaped soundholes. Rest of body consists of rectangular cigar box, of 'cigar box cedar', stamped with a trade name (now illegible) on the base, and with *Flor Fina* on the end. Sides of the box decorated with applied motifs of a black synthetic resin, their star-shaped centres filled with some form of plaster. Neck and crudely carved anthropomorphic head of mahogany, with decorative varnished finish and the initials CH applied in metal at each side of the head. Single wire string held by ebony peg at back of neck. Small circular nut of ebony and 22 frets cut into the neck. Made by donor's father. In own home-made canvas case.

Dimensions   Total length 850mm, width 108mm, depth 93mm, string length 765mm.

Provenance   Presented by Mrs E. Wilson, 1958.

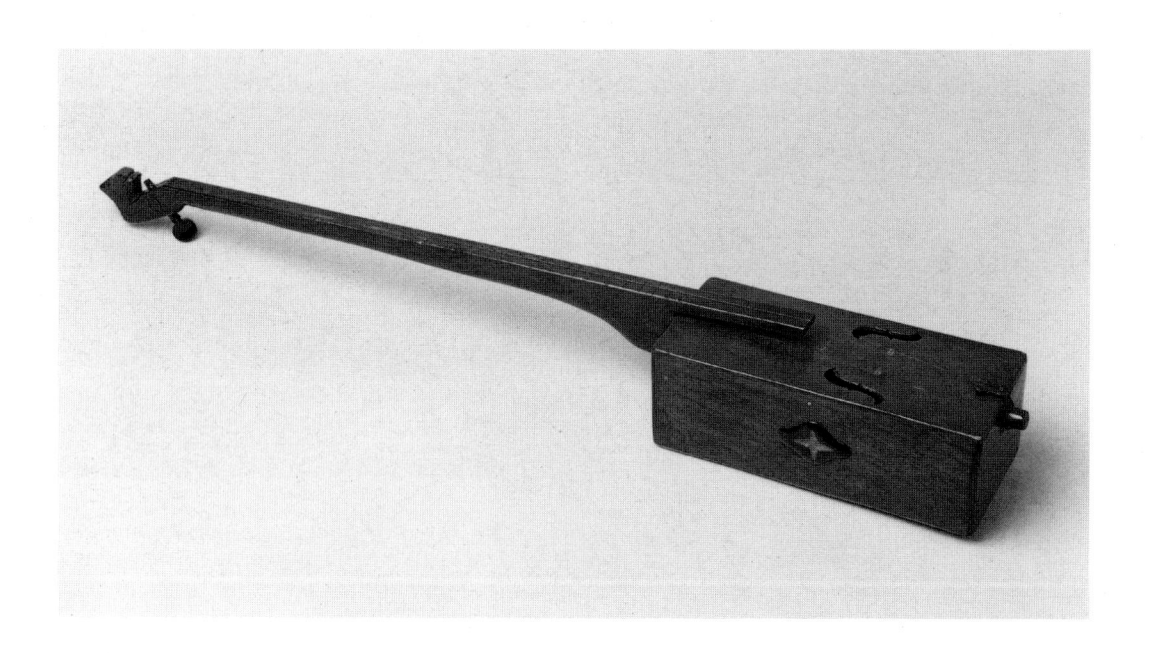

5.26. STROVIOL, unsigned, *c*.1920–1930

Museum Accession Number 1969.201.1

Label *Concert Hall Model, Stroviols, Trade Mark, Registered, British Manufacture* on metal label.

Body of mahogany with two steel brackets at one end. Ebonised fingerboard with synthetic ivory nut, eight inlaid synthetic ivory frets and six brass fret markers. Single metal string held by ebony button and single ebony peg in the head. Chrome-plated horn. In own canvas case.

Dimensions Total length 880mm, depth of body 110mm, length of horn 403mm, diameter of bell 188mm.

Provenance Presented by Mrs Batterson, 1969.

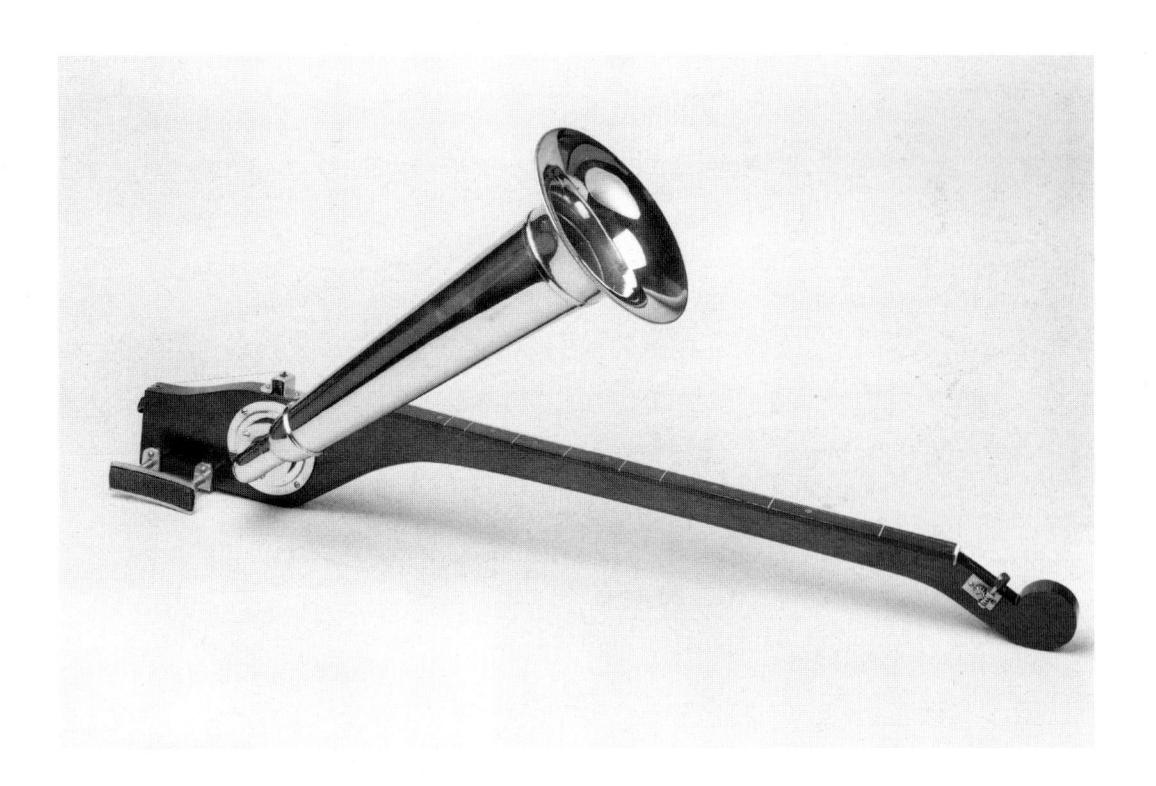

5.27. KIT BOW, Dodd, eighteenth century

Museum Accession Number 1967.161.35a

Stamp	*Dodd*, on the frog.
	Rosewood stick of circular section, with ivory frog and ball-shaped ivory screw cap. In own, later, case of mahogany lined with red velvet.
Dimensions	Total length 443mm, width 25mm.
Maker	This bow could have been made by Edward Dodd (1705–1810), or by his son, the more famous John Dodd (*c*.1752–1839), who is regarded as one of the greatest English bow makers.
Provenance	Rushworth and Dreaper Ltd, Liverpool, –1967.
References	Bevan, 1990, p.68.

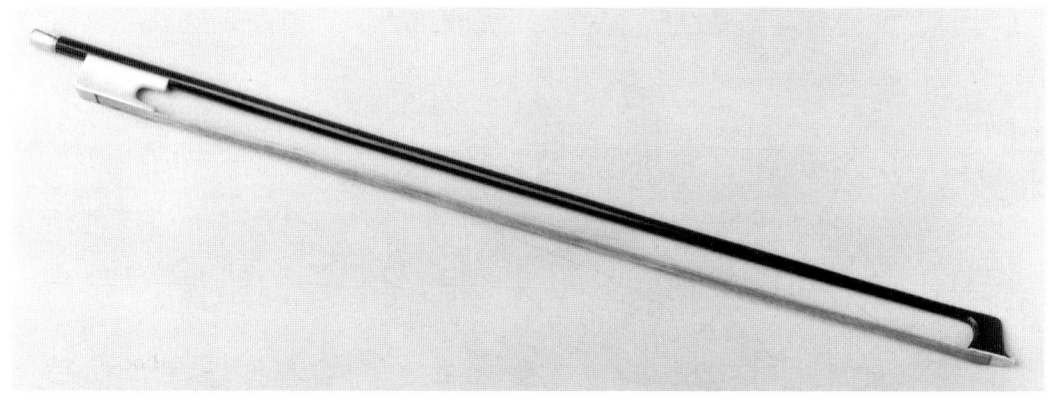

5.27

5.28. VIOLIN BOW, Jean-Baptiste Vuillaume, Paris, nineteenth century

Museum Accession Number 1967.161.41

Stamp	*Vuillaume A Paris, Brevete Invention* on top of stick.
	Steel stick of circular section, with ebony frog and silver-plated ferrule, the decorative inlay now missing, and ebony and silver screw cap with abilone shell inlay in top.
Dimensions	Total length 756mm.
Maker	Jean-Baptiste Vuillaume (1798–1875) was one of the best-known of all nineteenth-century violin makers and dealers. Based in Paris for most of his working life, he both made his own instruments, many of them close copies of eighteenth-century examples, and dealt in old ones. A number of different craftsmen produced the bows stamped with his name.
Provenance	Rushworth and Dreaper Ltd, Liverpool, –1967.

5.29. SIX VIOLIN BOWS, nineteenth century

Museum Accession Number 1967.161.42

a. Unsigned.

Mahogany stick of circular section, with mahogany frog and circular ivory screw cap.

Dimensions Total length 717mm.

b. Unsigned.

Mahogany stick of circular section, with ivory frog and octagonal ivory screw cap.

Dimensions Total length 700mm.

c.

Stamp *Betts* on frog.

Mahogany stick of circular section, with ivory frog and circular, flat-headed ivory screw cap.

Dimensions Total length 717mm.

d. Unsigned.

Mahogany stick of circular section, with ivory frog and octagonal ivory screw cap.

Dimensions Total length 690mm.

e. Unsigned.

Rosewood stick of circular section, with ebony frog and fruitwood (?) screw cap.

Dimensions Total length 717mm.

f. Unsigned.

Rosewood stick of octagonal section, with decorative fluting, rosewood frog and screw cap.

Dimensions Total length 705mm.

5.30. HURDY-GURDY, Pierre Tixier, Jenzat, France, c.1850–1860

Museum Accession Number 1967.161.45

Stamp *Tixier A Janzat* within a flowerhead on the side of the keybox.

Lute-shaped body composed of nine alternately-stained sycamore ribs. Belly of two pieces of pine, painted around the edge with a wavy decorative line in red, and inlaid with a band of alternating bone and dark-stained wood, with boxwood stringing and inlay. Pegbox of sycamore, the hinged lid and the tailpiece both veneered with rosewood and inlaid with mother-of-pearl floral motifs and boxwood stringing. Bridge of beech. Ten keys of bone and 13 of ebony. Carved head and pegbox of sycamore, stained red at the sides. Six gut strings held by six ebony pegs. Set of four metal 'sympathetic' strings on the right-hand side, on a small ebony bridge, held by steel wrest pins. Wheel-guard veneered with rosewood and inlaid with boxwood stringing and scrolling floral pattern in boxwood and stained wood. Iron crank with ivory knob. Small knob for holding trompette string now missing.

Dimensions Total length 740mm, width 328mm, string length 360mm.

Maker Pierre Tixier (1829–1887) was one of many hurdy-gurdy makers working in Jenzat, the most prominant area for the making of these instruments during the nineteenth century.

Provenance Charles van Raalte, Brownsea Island, Dorset, –1925.
Sir Arthur Wheeler, Brownsea Island, Dorset, 1925–1927.
Rushworth and Dreaper Ltd, Liverpool, 1927–1967.

Rushworth and Dreaper purchased this instrument from Sir Arthur Wheeler of Brownsea Castle, Brownsea Island, on 21st June, 1927, for the sum of £4.10.0.

References R & D catalogue 1 (undated), not paginated.
R & D catalogue 2 (undated), p.10.
Sale catalogue, Fox and Sons, 1927, p.104, lot 1725.
Whittington-Egan, 1976, pp.157–158.
Bevan, 1990, p.68.

5.31. PHILOMELE (Bowed Zither), unsigned, probably Austrian, *c.*1850

Museum Accession Number 1967.161.34

Unsigned.

Belly of a single piece of pine, with two flame-shaped soundholes, inlaid around the outer edge with boxwood stringing and with a band of alternating boxwood and ebony. Flat back of a single piece of sycamore. Sides, neck and head, the latter carved in the form of a lion's head, all of sycamore. Fingerboard of a lighter wood, with open carved decoration at bridge end. Nut and bridge of ebony, the bridge with an inlaid strip of brass across the top. Four strings, two steel and two overspun, held by pins in the bridge and by four rosewood pegs in the head.

Dimensions Total length 610mm, width of bouts 172mm, 106mm, 230mm, depth 35mm, string length from nut to bridge 342mm.

Provenance Paul de Wit, Leipzig, –1922.
Rushworth and Dreaper Ltd, Liverpool, 1922–1967.

A note in the archives of Rushworth and Dreaper states that they bought this instrument from Paul de Wit on 12th September, 1922. The cost was 25 shillings, plus carriage and (import ?) duty, bringing the final cost to 35 shillings.

5.32. GUSLE AND BOW, Serbian, nineteenth century

Museum Accession Number 56.28.383

Unsigned.

Belly of calfskin, with nine holes pierced in the centre, stretched over wooden frame and secured with wooden nails. Head, neck and back composed of single piece of sycamore, decorated all over with small circular scorch marks, the back shaped and painted in five 'ribs' with scrolling floral design in black and red, the central 'rib' pierced with a cross-shaped hole. Carved head, resembling that of a horse, the flat front of the head painted with floral decoration and a 'pseudo' shield of arms in red and green. Single thick black horsehair string, held by large carved wooden peg through the top of the neck. Curved bow of sycamore with single thick string of black horsehair.

Dimensions Total length 650mm, width 183mm, length of bow 525mm, width of bow 148mm.

Provenance Presented by Miss Irby, 1956.

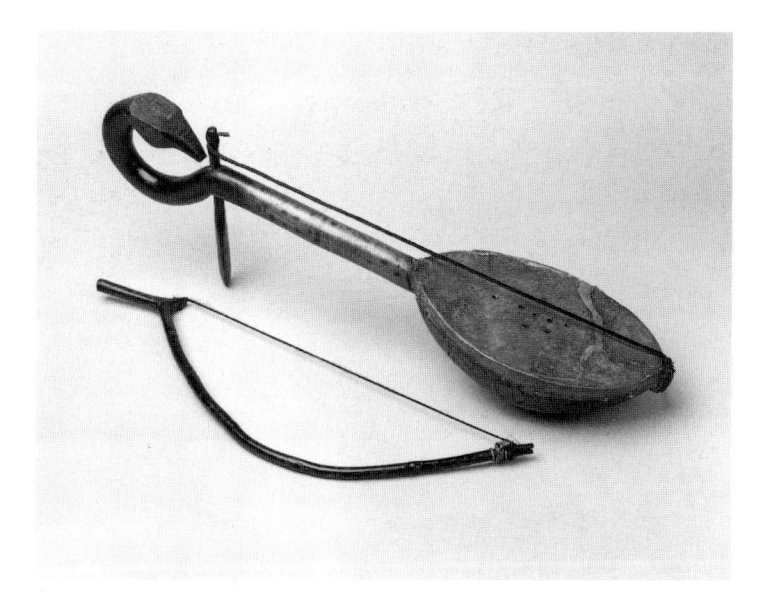

Detail

5.33. CRWTH, George Hemmings, Liverpool, 1959

Museum Accession Number 1967.161.38

Unsigned.

Belly of a single piece of pine, with two small circular soundholes. Bridge of beech, with right-hand foot passing through right-hand soundhole and resting on inside back, forming the sound-post. Back, sides, arms and neck of sycamore. Fingerboard of a lighter wood, extending out over the belly. Tailpiece of horn. Ebony nut and four gut strings, held by four steel wrestpins.

Dimensions — Total length 585mm, length of belly 315mm, width 230mm, depth 53mm, string length from nut to tailpiece 438mm.

Provenance — Rushworth and Dreaper Ltd, Liverpool, 1959–1967.

This instrument was made in August 1959 by George Hemmings, Senior Luthier at Rushworth and Dreaper, as a reproduction of the eighteenth-century crwth in the collection of Warrington Museum.

References — Bevan, 1990, p.69.

Percussion Instruments

6.1. TAMBOURINE, unsigned, late nineteenth century

Museum Accession Number 57.151.2

Unsigned.

Wooden frame, completely covered with painted cotton sateen on the front, pale green cotton velvet around the edge and plain, natural-coloured cotton fabric on the back. Front decorated with a design of crysanthemums in oils. Six pairs of copper alloy jingles around the frame. Large pink silk bow attached to edge at bottom, two pink silk bows at top, their long ends joined to form a carrying handle or hanging strap.

Dimensions   Diameter 360mm, depth 65mm.

Provenance   Presented by Miss F. Arthur, 1957.

6.2. CASTANETS, unsigned, probably Spanish, late nineteenth century

Museum Accession Number 60.180. 5 & 6

Unsigned.

Two pairs of castanets, both of lignum vitae, one set with the remains of red silk cord with which they were joined, the other set without.

Dimensions Length 77mm, diameter 57mm.

Provenance Presented by Mr D. Jones, 1960.

Mechanical Instruments

PLAYER PIANOS

7.1. PUSH-UP PIANO PLAYER, Melville Clark, Chicago, c.1899–1905

Museum Accession Number 60.41

TECHNICAL SPECIFICATION

Serial Number	9263
Roll-box Inscription	*Melville Clark* *Chicago–New York – London* *APOLLO*
Compass	58 Notes, by maple transposing Tracker-Bar
Action	Pneumatic
Stops	Roll-drive control by single knob: Rewind / Off / Slow / Medium / Fast
	Two buttons pneumatically operating the two pedals on the piano
Case Size	Height 1010mm, Width 1005mm, Depth 450mm
Maker	Melville Clark (*c.*1890–*c.*1940)

DESCRIPTION

This instrument was an early form of piano player. It was 'pushed up' against the keys of a piano and, when pedalled, activated them and played it. The rectangular case, on metal castors, is veneered all over with rosewood. The case front is decorated on both sides with a carved, stylised flower head and a long palmette, above three grooved lines. Two long, narrow doors in the lower section of the case conceal the pedals, with rubber-covered treads.

The roll compartment in the top of the case is concealed by a folding lid, the interior veneered with bird's-eye maple. The *Soft pedal/Loud pedal* buttons are positioned on the left-hand side of this compartment. In the centre is the transposing tracker-bar, of maple, with transposer knob on the left for changing the key, marked *Transposing Regulator*. The tracker-bar has 58 air vents along the top. When the music-roll passed over the tracker-bar and a perforation in it coincided with one of these vents, air was drawn down by suction from the pedal pump. This activated a pneumatic valve, causing a miniature bellows to move a striker-knob or 'finger' onto the relevant piano key. The clockwork mechanism for the roll drive is also situated on the top of the case, concealed by a hinged cover to the right of the roll compartment. The roll drive was wound through a friction clutch by cranks from the pedals and was controlled by a pair of concentric levers on the right-hand side. These are marked *Rewind/Off/Slow/Medium/Fast*. The inner lever controls the rewind and the outer controls the speed. The speed is regulated by a centrifugal governor, which moves a disc brake against a friction pad attached to the outer lever.

The back of the case houses the rows of felt-covered wooden striker-knobs or 'fingers' in the upper section. In the lower section there are two wooden castors for adjusting the height of the case to the piano keys.

John Griffiths

HISTORY OF THE INSTRUMENT

Provenance Presented by Mr F.C. Brailsford, 1960.

The early history of this particular instrument is unknown. The maker, Melville Clark, was one of the first to develop and produce player pianos and their *Apollo* model was introduced in 1899.

7.2. PIANOLA, George Steck, for the Aeolian Company, U.S.A., *c.*1930

Museum Accession Number 1989.35

TECHNICAL SPECIFICATION

Serial Numbers   100463, S10243, 14698

Nameboard Inscription   *Steck* / *'Pianola' Piano*

Retailer's Inscription   *Piano Makers to the late Queen Victoria Sole agents James Smith & Son / Music Sellers Ltd 76–70 Lord St / Liverpool Southport & Warrington*

Compass   7 Octaves, AAA – a^4

3-Octave-Span   494mm. Ivory naturals, ebony sharps

Stringing   15 singles – b^1, 13 bi-chords – c, trichord – a^4
Overstrung. Full cast frame

	AAA	c^2	a^4
Scaling	1105mm	344mm	57mm
Strike-Point	150mm	40mm	4mm
Gauges Extant	6.68mm (spun)	0.94mm	0.76mm

Piano Action   Tape-check. Dampers to c^3

Player Action   Aeolian 88 note
Foot pumped
Pneumatic expression control. Bass/Treble split at c^1
Triple-paired roll-drive motor
Tracking control by roll edge fingers

Piano Stops   2 pedals: Piano by half-blow
                                 Damper lift

Player Stops   7 handstops: Half-blow
                                  Dampers
                                  Expression bass
                                  Expression treble
                                  Keyboard clamp
                                  Tempo
                                  Re-roll

Case size   Height 1225mm, Width 1490mm, Depth 740mm

Maker   George Steck for the Aeolian Company (1903–1931)

Retailer   James Smith and Son (*c.*1830–*c.*1958)

DESCRIPTION   The case is of ebonised wood, with a highly polished finish all over. There are two plain panels with beaded edgings to each side of the central compartment for rolls, which closes with a sliding door. The pedal mechanism and pedals, with ridged rubber treads, are

concealed by a folding door beneath the keyboard.
With matching rectangular pianola stool, with upholstered lid and adjustable support inside to create sloping seat for pedalling pianola pedals. Contains 35 boxed pianola rolls.

HISTORY OF THE INSTRUMENT

Provenance Presented by Mr Hodson, 1989.

This instrument was in the donor's family for many years and was probably bought as new.
  The Aeolian Company was founded originally as the Aeolian Organ and Music Co., in New York in 1888 by William B. Tremaine. His son, Harry Tremaine formed the Aeolian, Weber Piano and Pianola Co. in 1903. It became the parent body for a large number of smaller firms, including George Steck. It continued in business under the name Aeolian Co. until 1931 when it was taken over by the Ernest M. Skinner Company. The retailer of the instrument, James Smith and Son, was a long-established Liverpool firm, trading in Bold Street from about 1830 until the 1950s.

BARREL ORGANS

7.3. BARREL ORGAN, William Phillips, London, early nineteenth century

Museum Accession Number 1967.161.3

Label — *Patent Piano Fortes with Drum and Triangle, W. Phillips, Piano Forte & Organ Manufacturer, Music Seller, Printer & Publisher, Corner of Manor Row, facing the bottom of the Minories & Little Tower Hill, London. A large and fashionable assortment of Improved Patent Piano Fortes, Barrel Organs, Guitars, Tambourines, Triangles, Patent Flutes, Flageolets and every other article in the Musical Branch* on paper label on underside of lid.

Back and interior of case of pine, front, sides and lid of solid mahogany. Central section of case veneered with crossbanded mahogany and inlaid with bands of a lighter wood, possibly sycamore. Oval-shaped opening in central section, with nine flat-backed dummy pipes of gilt wood, backed with pale green silk. Painted oval cartouche and three gilt metal stop-knobs, on wooden shanks, marked *Diapason, Principal, Triangle*. Mechanism wound by brass and hardwood handle on right-hand side of case front.

Wooden pinned barrel, set of bellows in base and two ranks of pipes, 14 wooden and 14 lead (three of these now missing). Triangle attachment. Plays 10 tunes.

Case set into mahogany stand, inlaid with decorative border of lighter woods, with four tapering legs and drawer in base for storing extra barrel (now missing).

Dimensions — Height 1210mm, width 540mm, depth 384mm.

Maker — William Phillips is first listed in Kent's Directory of 1803 at 8 Manor Row, Little Tower Hill, London. In 1805 he moved to 9 Manor Row and was last listed in Robson's Directory for 1828–29.

Provenance — Mr R.F. Mathison, –1957.
Rushworth and Dreaper Ltd, Liverpool, 1957–1967.

This instrument was presented to Rushworth and Dreaper by a Mr Mathison of Liverpool. It had originally belonged to his grandfather.

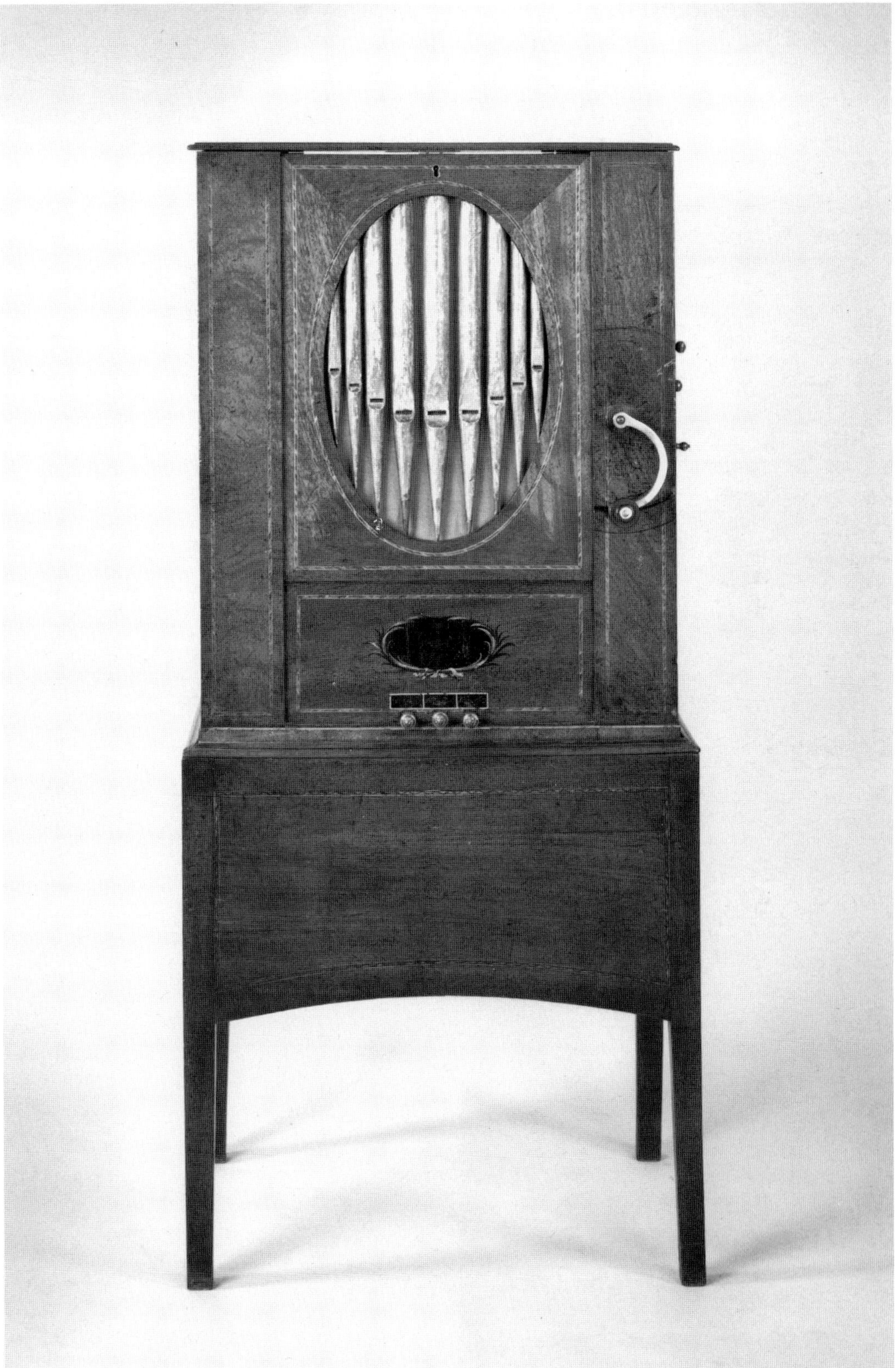

7.4. CHURCH BARREL ORGAN, T.C. Bates and Son, London, *c.*1835–1840

Museum Accession Number 1967.161.2

Label *T.C.Bates & Son, Organ Builders, 6 Ludgate Hill, London* on paper label on front of case.

Tall case of oak panels, the centre front panel of the lower half of the case lifting out to allow access to the interior. Upper half of case front divided into three sections, with seven flat-backed, gilt wooden dummy pipes in the central section and five in each of the side sections, all backed with modern blue cotton fabric. Top of each section carved as Gothic-shaped arch, with ogee decoration, stylised Gothic leaves and central motif.

Three pinned wooden barrels, painted pink, pale blue and yellow, each one labelled *T.C. Bates & Son, Organ Builders, 6 Ludgate Hill, London*, and playing 10 hymns each. Clockwork drive to the barrels via a worm and wheel. Five ranks of pipes, (45 lead alloy and 27 wood in total) and five stops, marked *Fifteenth, Principal, Stopped Diapason, Open Diapason, Bourdon* on ivory stop-knobs. Foot pedal for bellows at back of case.

Dimensions Height 2890mm, width 1195mm, depth 760mm.

Maker T.C. Bates appears in the London trade directories at Ludgate Hill from 1835, listed as an organ-builder and piano-forte maker. In 1839 he acquired additional premises in Dorset Street, where he is listed as a music-seller. He disappears from the directories altogether after 1845.

Provenance Rushworth and Dreaper Ltd, Liverpool, 1926–1967

This instrument was purchased by Rushworth and Dreaper from 'Bedwell, G.C.' (?) on 4th May, 1926, at a cost of £25. 'Organ works' totalling a further £5 were carried out on the instrument after purchase.

References R & D catalogue 1 (undated), not paginated.
R & D catalogue 2 (undated), p.8.
The Liverpolitan, 1937, p.15.
Bevan, 1990, p.68.

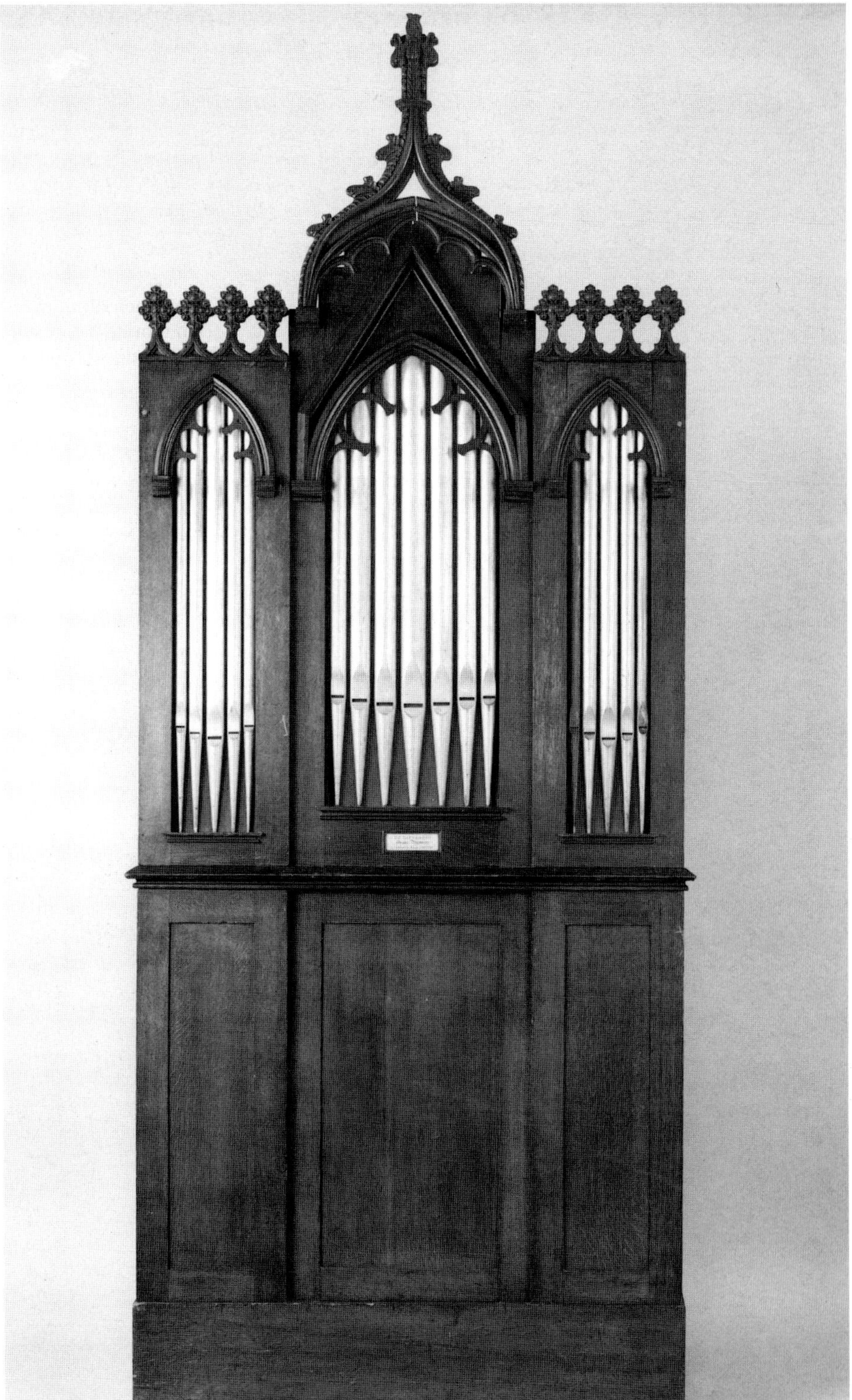

7.5. BARREL ORGAN, unsigned, probably German, c.1860

Museum Accession Number 59.146

Label	*R.J. Ward & Son, Musical Instrument Maker, 10 St Anne Street, Islington, Liverpool* on oval ceramic label on lid, and *Ward & Son, Musical Instrument Makers, Liverpool / From Ward and Sons' Musical Instrument Manufactory, 10 St Anne Street, Islington, Liverpool, Concertinas, Accordions, Flutinas, Violins, Guitars, Banjoes, Violin and Banjo strings, etc etc* on paper label on top of bellows.
Inscription	*Bought by Austin Johnson, 31 Fairview Road, Oxton, Birkenhead, 1935* in ink, and batch number *5757* in pencil, both on front of reservoir.
	Rectangular case of poplar, decorated on front, back, sides and underside of lid with 'combed' varnished finish. Lid decorated with applied transfer print depicting two birds protecting nest of eggs from attacking snake, surrounded by transfer-printed border of silver and green vine leaves. Single wooden barrel, turned by a worm and wheel, and set of bellows activated by a crank at front of case. Top of bellows covered with wood-effect paper. Beech tracker-rod for changing tunes, its end emerging as handle at right-hand side of case. Twenty-two brass reeds in base of case, below bellows.
Dimensions	Height 285mm, width 585mm, depth 290mm.
Provenance	Purchased from Leicester Museum, 1959.

7.6. SERAPHONE, the English Automatic Seraphone Company, *c.*1880

Museum Accession Number 52.113

Label *The English Automatic Seraphone Company*, with instructions for playing, on label on underside of lid.

Square case of mahogany, with varnished pine interior, on ebonised base, the front and sides decorated with stylised flowers and border in gold paint. Narrow, hinged flap in front of case pulls down to increase volume of sound. Central lid opens to reveal winding mechanism for the two wooden rolls, on a pine base stamped with the serial number *1377*. Tracker-bar of beech with 20 air vents along the top. Bellows in bottom of case operated by wooden handle on right-hand side. Twenty brass reeds, each marked with its own note.

Dimensions Height 260mm, width 426mm, depth 310mm.

Provenance Presented by Mr F.G. Smeaton, 1952.

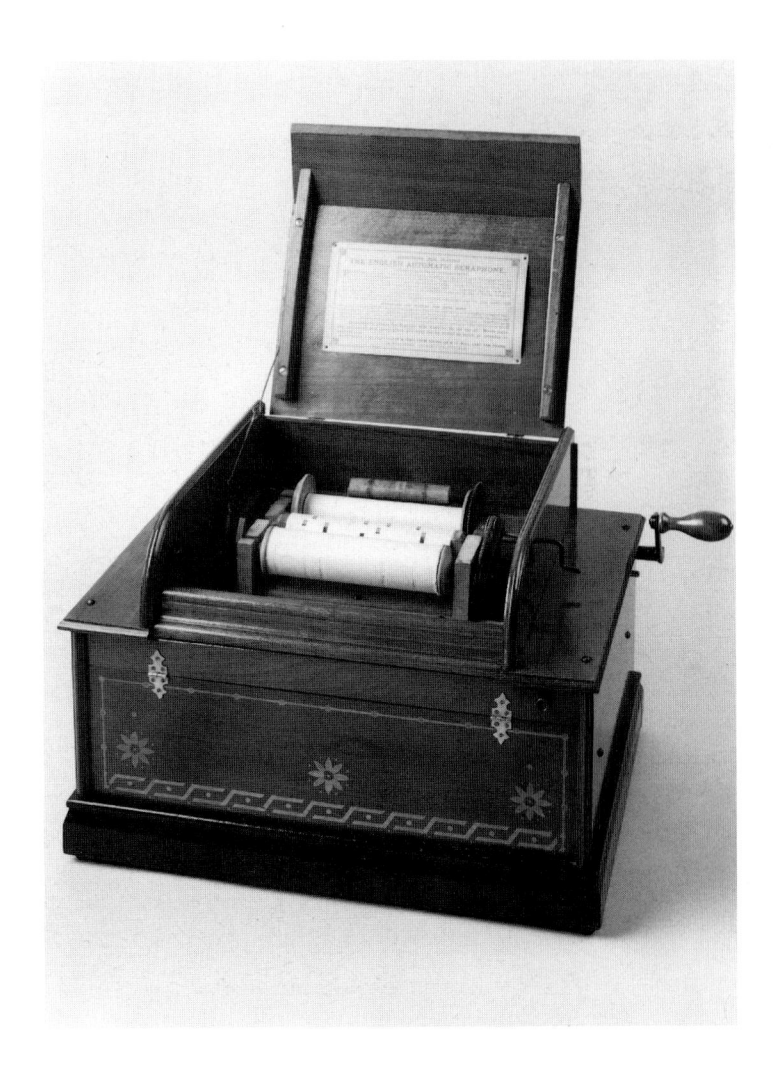

Musical Boxes and Polyphons

7.7. MUSICAL BOX, Lecoultre Frères, Geneva, *c*.1850

Museum Accession Number 1963.289.56

Stamp	*LF. Gve* on comb.
	Rectangular case, veneered all over with mahogany, the front, back and sides decorated with an applied, 'combed' varnish. Top of lid inlaid with four lines of light wood stringing. Interior of case stained red. Cylinder and comb, with key-wind mechanism on barrel on left hand side. Geneva stopwork mechanism missing from barrel. Speed governed by worm-driven fly on right-hand side. Three on/off/adjuster levers located on left-hand side, concealed by hinged left side of case. Narrow compartment on right-hand side of case holds wooden-handled key. Serial number *27450* stamped on brass bed plate. No glass cover. Plays six tunes, detailed on tune-sheet attached to underside of lid.
Dimensions	Height 110mm, width 400mm, depth 150mm.
Provenance	Presented by Mrs S. Swayne-Thomas, 1963.

7.8. MUSICAL BOX, Paillard, Vaucher, Fils, Ste Croix, Switzerland, *c.*1870

Museum Accession Number 55.97

Stamp	PVF on the stop/start lever plate.
	Rectangular case, the front, sides and back painted and varnished to resemble rosewood, the lid veneered with walnut, inlaid with a central cartouche of a winged cherub driving a chariot pulled by a butterfly, in pale and stained fruitwoods and abilone shell on a dark stained sycamore ground. Central lid motif bordered by three bands of fruitwood stringing.
	Interior of case ebonised. Cylinder and comb, with ratcheted lever-winding mechanism on left-hand side and stop/start levers on right. Geneva stopwork mechanism on barrel. Speed governed by worm-driven fly on right-hand side. Glass cover. Plays six Scottish tunes, described on paper tune-sheet on underside of lid, printed with *Ste Croix (Suisse) PVF.*
Dimensions	Width 435mm, depth 192mm, height 140mm.
Maker	Paillard, Vaucher, Fils, known as PVF, were established in St Croix in 1814 as E. Paillard and Co. They were also known as Amedee Paillard and C. Paillard and Co., but were most famous as PVF, manufacturing musical boxes until about 1914.
Provenance	Presented by Miss Hilda Watson, 1955.

7.9. MUSICAL BOX, unsigned, Swiss, *c.*1870–1880

Museum Accession Number 61.70

Unsigned.

Rectangular case, the front and sides veneered with rosewood, crossbanded with tulipwood and bordered with a light wood stringing. Back veneered with plain rosewood. Case front decorated with applied ormolu escutcheon in form of a grotesque head surrounded by scrolling foliage. Lid also veneered with rosewood, crossbanded with tulipwood, bordered with a light wood stringing, and inlaid with central cartouche of winged cherub blowing a horn, in pale and stained fruitwoods.

Interior of case ebonised. Cylinder and comb, with ratcheted lever-winding mechanism on left-hand side and stop/start levers on right. Geneva stopwork mechanism missing from barrel. Speed governed by worm-driven fly (damaged). Silver-plated zither attachment, its control lever set in silver-plated lyre-shaped mount. Nine engraved bells, four of them struck by hammers in the form of gilt metal wasps or bees, the others by plain hammers. Glass cover. Plays 12 tunes from various operas, described on paper tune-sheet attached to underside of lid, printed with the British Royal Arms, believed to be the trademark of *George Bendon & Co., London*, importers of Swiss musical boxes. Case raised on four ebonised corner feet.

Dimensions Width 730mm, depth 310mm, height 275mm.

Provenance Presented by Mrs A. Minton, 1961.

7.10. MUSICAL BOX, unsigned, *c.*1880

Museum Accession Number 1965.192

Unsigned.

Rectangular case, the front and sides veneered with walnut, crossbanded with tulipwood and bordered with a light wood stringing. Back of ebonised wood. Front inlaid with scrolling design of a ribbon hung with flowers, in a pale wood. Cast gilt bronze handles applied at the sides. Lid veneered with walnut, crossbanded with tulipwood, bordered with a light wood stringing, and inlaid with central design of gun, quiver of arrows and bird, surrounded by scrolling ribbon intertwined with flowers, all in pale and stained fruitwoods. Lid of box has been attached upside down, so central motif appears upside down.

   Interior of case ebonised. Cylinder and comb, with ratcheted lever-winding mechanism on left-hand side and stop/start levers on right. Geneva stopwork mechanism on barrel. Speed governed by worm-driven fly on right. Six engraved bells struck by hammers in the form of six golden birds. Glass cover. Plays 12 tunes, described on paper tune-sheet on underside of lid, printed with the British Royal Arms, believed to be the trademark of *George Bendon & Co., London*, importers of Swiss musical boxes. Case raised on four ebonised corner feet.

Dimensions	Width 695mm, depth 290mm, height 250mm.
Provenance	Purchased from Mr J.C. Mason, 1965.

7.11. MUSICAL BOX, unsigned, Swiss, *c.*1880

Museum Accession Number 1967.161.18

Label *Rushworth and Dreaper, Liverpool, Birkenhead, Chester & Southport* on label inside case, centre back.

Rectangular case, the front, back and sides painted and varnished to resemble kingwood, the lid veneered with rosewood. Top of lid inlaid with three shawms, tambourine and floral sprays in various pale and stained fruitwoods, surrounded by three inlaid lines of stringing in a lighter wood. Two fixed, cast-brass carrying handles attached at either side of case.

Interior of case ebonised. Cylinder and comb, with ratcheted lever-winding mechanism on left-hand side and stop/start levers on right. Geneva stopwork mechanism on barrel. Speed governed by worm-driven fly on right. Nine engraved bells, struck by plain metal hammers. Serial number *12210* stamped on brass bed plate. Glass cover. Plays 10 tunes. Tune-sheet now missing. Case raised on four ebonised corner feet.

Dimensions Height 255mm, width 555mm, depth 310mm.

Provenance Rushworth and Dreaper Ltd, Liverpool, –1967.

7.12. MUSICAL SNUFF BOX, unsigned, *c.*1880

Museum Accession Number 46.35.51

Unsigned.

Rectangular case of red japanned iron, the lid decorated with a black transfer-printed scene of three horsemen, dressed in the costume of the 1830s, riding along an Alpine lakeside. Interior of case, with sloping, shallow depression for snuff, painted gold. Key-wind clockwork mechanism in base, with stop/start button on front of case and tune-changer button on left-hand side. Geneva stopwork mechanism on barrel. Speed governed by worm-driven fly.

Dimensions Width 105mm, depth 64mm, height 32mm.

Provenance Presented by Mrs N.L. Coltart, 1946.

7.13. MUSICAL BOX, Paillard, Vaucher, Fils, Ste Croix, Switzerland, *c.*1890

Museum Accession Number 61.69

Stamp	*PVF* on either end of zither attachment and on stop/start lever plate.
	Rectangular case, the front, back and sides painted and varnished to resemble rosewood, lid veneered with mahogany, inlaid with central cartouche of stylised flowers in pale and stained fruitwoods on dark stained ground, and bordered with three bands of light wood stringing. Interior of case ebonised. Cylinder and comb, with ratcheted lever-winding mechanism on left-hand side and stop/start levers on right. Geneva stopwork mechanism on barrel. Speed governed by worm-driven fly on right. Nickel-plated zither attachment, its control lever set into shield-shaped mount engraved with lyre, tambourine and pan pipes. Glass cover. Plays 10 tunes, described in French and German on paper tune-sheet attached to underside of lid, printed with *PVF Ste Croix Suisse*.
Dimensions	Width 570mm, depth 208mm, height 140mm.
Provenance	Presented by Mr M.B. Manson, 1961.

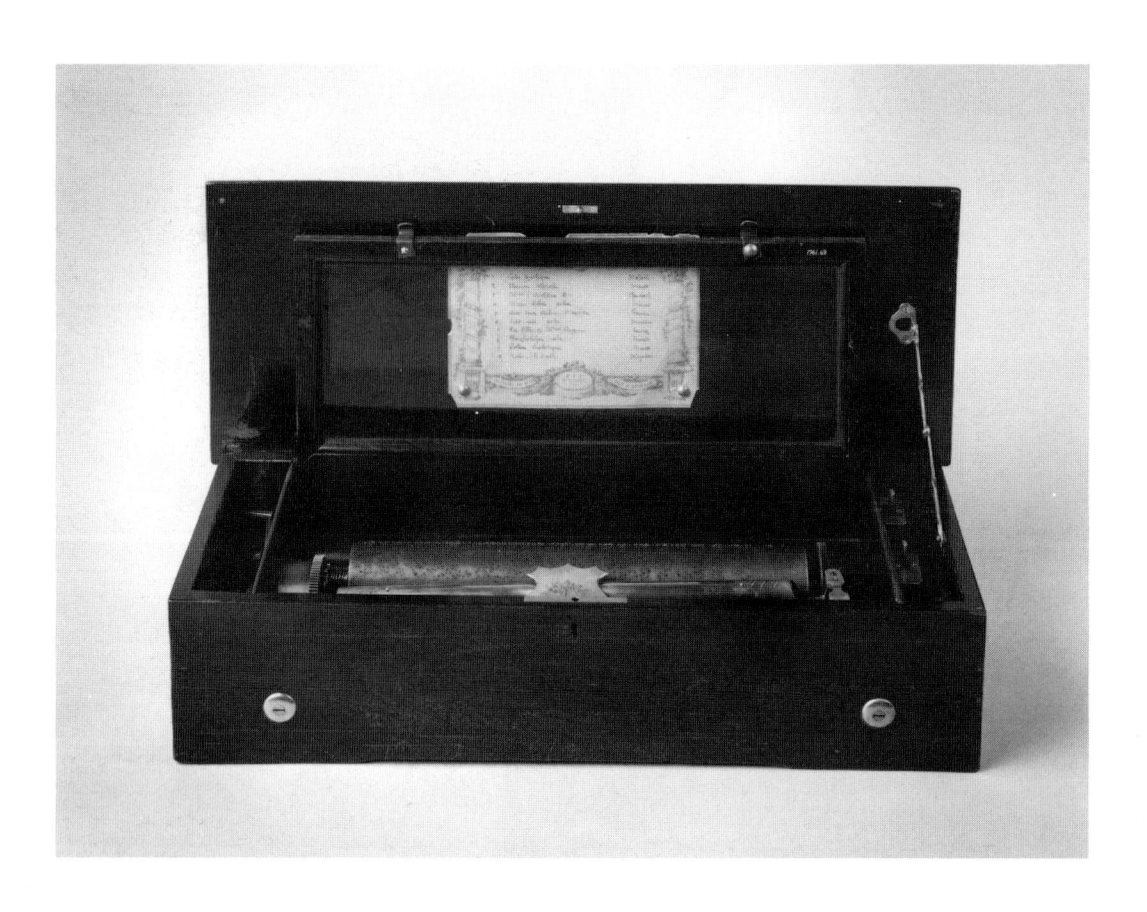

7.14. MINIATURE MUSICAL BOX, unsigned, Swiss, c.1890

Museum Accession Number 1967.161.17

Unsigned.

Rectangular case, veneered all over with bird's-eye maple, the outer edge of the lid and the corners crossbanded with mahogany. Top of lid inlaid with a bone shield. Interior of case ebonised. Small cylinder and comb and clockwork mechanism, activated by keywind on base of case. Geneva stopwork mechanism missing from barrel. Speed governed by worm-driven fly on left-hand side. Fixed glass cover. Plays six tunes, detailed on tune-sheet attached to underside of lid. Stands on four small brass ball feet.

Dimensions Height 44mm, width 128mm, depth 85mm.

Provenance Rushworth and Dreaper Ltd, Liverpool, −1967.

7.15. ORCHESTRAL MUSICAL BOX, B. A. Bremond and Co., Switzerland, *c.*1885–1890

Museum Accession Number 1967.161.19

Stamp *B.A. Bremond, Manufacturer, Geneva, No.17912* on brass tune-selection plate inside case.

Large rectangular case of ebonised wood, veneered on front and sides, top and underside of lid with panels of burr walnut edged with a light wood stringing, crossbanded with tulipwood.

Interior of case ebonised, the front section decorated with scrolling fretwork design, backed with modern yellow silk fabric. Double tandem barrels, wound by means of a detachable crank on left side of case, both barrels fitted with a Geneva stopwork mechanism and mounted on a common arbor. Speed governed by a worm-driven centrifugal fly on the left-hand side. Large cylinder, released by a thumb lever at each side, with three combs, the central one controlling the bells and drum. Four brass levers in front of combs engage and disengage the drum, bells and organ. Stop/start levers located on right-hand side. Twelve bells, with hammers in the form of enamelled metal butterflies and bees. Thirteen organ pipes and 22 reeds, activated by set of bellows below the metal bed plate. Glass cover, the frame veneered with burr walnut and pierced in each corner with decorative scrolling pattern. Six interchangeable cylinders, each playing eight tunes, detailed on tune-sheet attached to underside of lid and printed *B.A. Bremond, Manufacturer, Place des Alpes, Geneva, No.17912*.

Stand, on four carved cabriole legs with metal castors, also of ebonised wood veneered with panels of burr walnut, crossbanded with tulipwood and inlaid with a light wood stringing. Chamfered corners of stand and 'knees' of legs carved with scrolling acanthus decoration. Two drawers in centre front of stand, concealed by a flap, their fronts veneered with a pale bird's-eye maple, with compartments for five extra cylinders.

Dimensions Height 1150mm, width 1420mm, depth 740mm.

Maker B. A. Bremond and Co (1860–*c.*1900 ?).

Provenance Rushworth and Dreaper Ltd, Liverpool –1967.

References Remnant, 1978, p.182, fig.163.

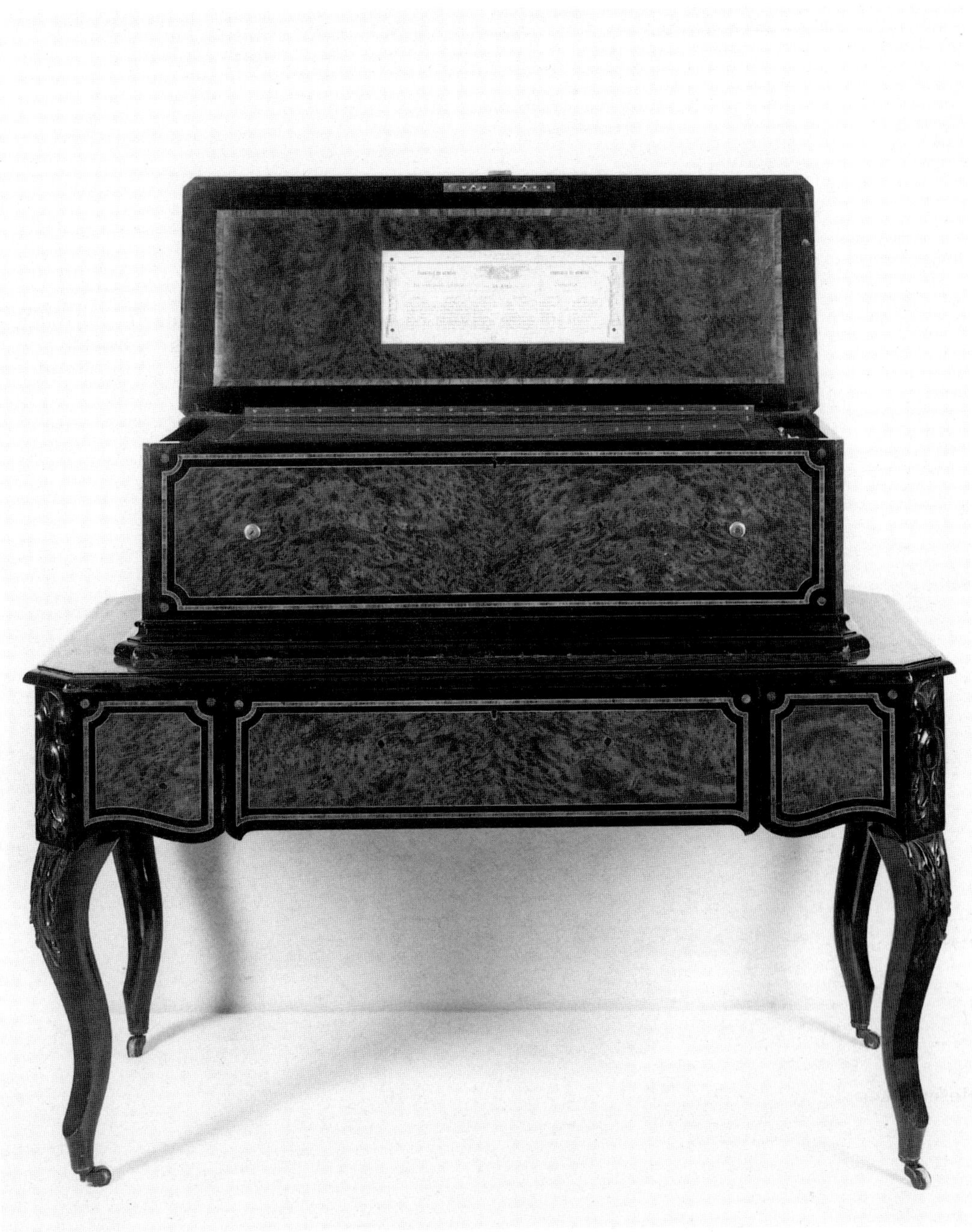

7.16. MUSICAL BOX, unsigned, Swiss, *c.*1900

Museum Accession Number 1967.37.2

Unsigned.

Rectangular case, the sides and back veneered with plain rosewood, the front and lid veneered with rosewood crossbanded with mahogany, bordered with fruitwood stringing. Lid inlaid with central motif of musical instruments (two shawms, a drum and pan-pipes) and flowers in pale and stained fruitwoods and boxwood.

Interior of case ebonised. Cylinder and comb, with ratcheted lever-winding mechanism on left-hand side and stop/start levers on right. Tandem barrels, with Geneva stopwork mechanism, on central arbor. Speed governed by worm-driven fly on right-hand side. Glass cover. Plays eight tunes. Tune-sheet now missing.

Dimensions — Width 565mm, depth 210mm, height 135mm.

Provenance — Presented by Mrs C. Elston, 1967.

7.17. POLYPHON, Polyphon Musikwerke, Leipzig, *c*.1895–1900

Museum Accession Number 1968.38

Unsigned.

Square case, the sides and lid veneered with walnut, the interior veneered with kingwood. Inside of lid decorated with sepia-coloured print, depicting putti playing various musical instruments in a scene of Classical ruins.

Single comb mechanism with centre drive, the metal bed plate stamped *POLYPHON*. Lever wound, the ratcheted lever and stop/start button positioned at front of case. With 27 original steel discs.

Dimensions Width 310mm, depth 280mm, height 160mm.

Maker Thousands of disc musical boxes of this kind were manufactured by the German firm of Polyphon Musikwerke, founded in Leipzig in 1886. They continued to produce them well into the early twentieth century.

Provenance Purchased from Mrs R. Hodge, 1968.

7.18. POLYPHON, Polyphon Musikwerke, Leipzig, 1897

Museum Accession Number 1970.68

Label *Polyphon / Automatic Musical Instrument / Made in Leipsic* on metal strip above door.

Stamp *William Lea, 50 & 52 Church St, Liverpool* in gold letters.

Case veneered with mahogany, crossbanded on the front door and decorated in the top corners with fretwork designs. Central window flanked at either side by a turned, baluster-shaped column. Top section decorated with a fan-shaped mount, flanked by turned finials. Large mainspring-driven mechanism, with date of manufacture stamped on it, enclosed in removable glass 'box' inside case and activated by handle at right-hand side. Speed governed by centrifugal fly. Single vertical comb on vertical metal bed plate. Slot for pennies and box to collect them located on right-hand side of case.

Case stands on square, mahogany-veneered cupboard, supported by two turned, bulbous 'feet' at front and by shaped wooden block at back. Cupboard has two doors, flanked by turned, baluster-shaped pilasters, and 12 interior divisions to hold the metal discs. Four turned feet. Case and cupboard may not be original match.

Dimensions Height (without baluster supports) 1860mm, width 690mm, depth 580mm.

Retailer William Lea first appears in the Liverpool trade directories in 1878, based at 56 & 58 Melville Place. He seems to have moved to Church Street by 1891 and to have continued in business there until around 1904, after which he moved to 124 Bold Street. He traded from Bold Street until 1938, after which date he disappears from the directories altogether.

Provenance Purchased from Mrs Florence Hitchins, 1970.

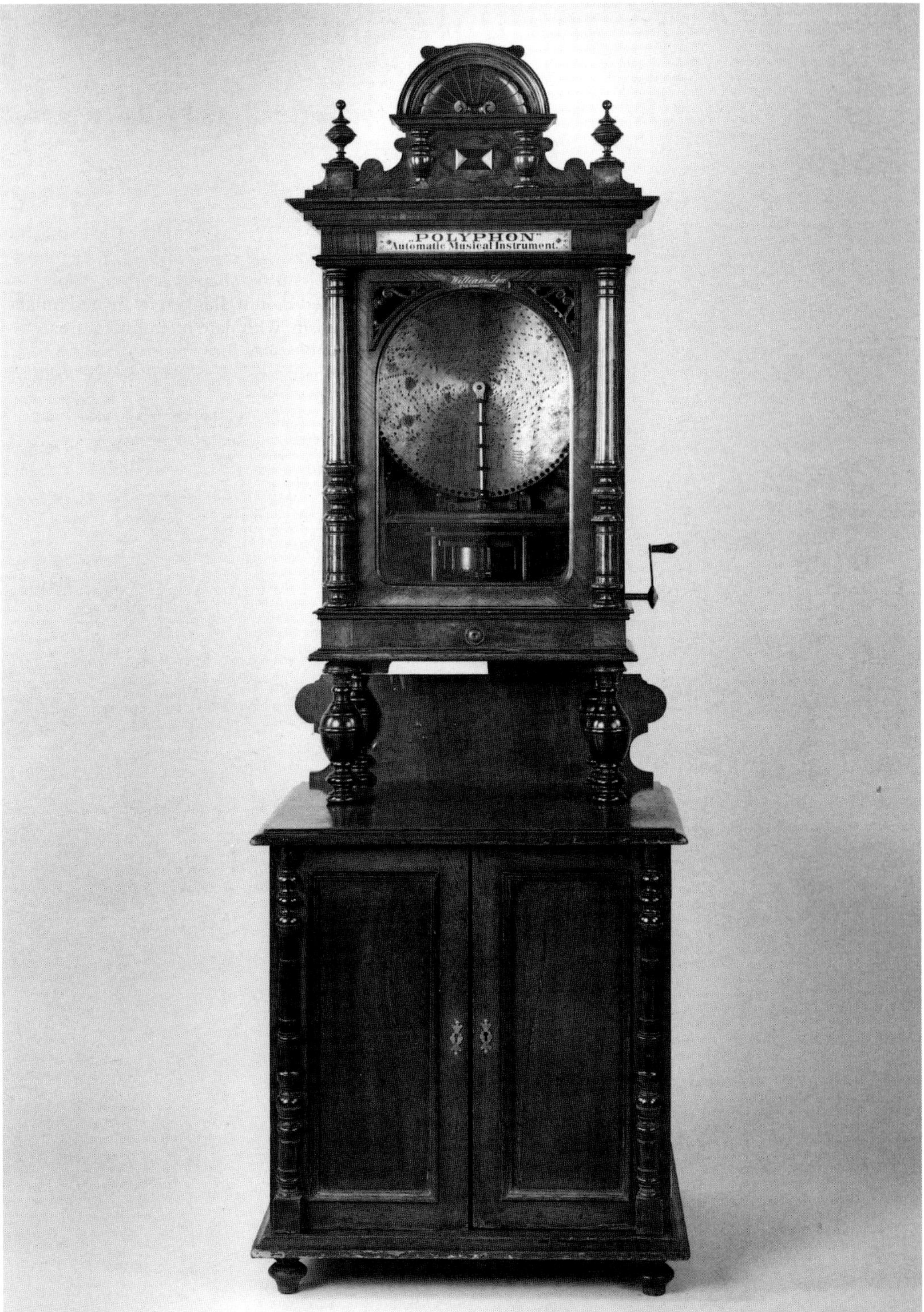
"POLYPHON"
Automatic Musical Instrument.

Automata

7.19. SINGING BIRD AUTOMATON, probably Bontems, Paris, *c*.1900

Museum Accession Number 62.15.42

Unsigned.

Bird in cage of gilt metal wire, with ring carrying handle, on base of carved gilt wood, decorated around the bottom with a band of moulded gesso in relief. Base of cage covered with gold-coloured crushed velvet. Bird on perch of brass tubing, a mounted North American Scarlet Tanager (*Piranga olivacea*).

   The bird's song is produced by means of a miniature whistle, the pitch varied by a piston, controlled by a cam, which varies the length of the whistle tube.

Dimensions   Height 540mm, diameter of base 300mm.

Maker   The firm of Bontems was founded around 1849 by the French clockmaker Blaise Bontems. The firm specialised in making singing bird automata and doll automata throughout the nineteenth century and were based at 72 rue de Clery, Paris. The business was finally bought by the firm of Reuge during the 1950s.

Provenance   Presented by Mr C. Whitthread, 1962.

BIBLIOGRAPHY

Baines, Anthony. 1966. *European and American Musical Instruments*, London.
Barnes, Alan. 1982. *An 18th Century English Organ Builder*, unpublished PhD thesis, University of Leicester.
Barnes, Alan and Renshaw, Martin (eds.). 1993. *The Life and Work of John Snetzler*, London.
Bevan, Clifford (ed.). 1990. *Musical Instrument Collections in the British Isles*, Winchester.
Blom, Eric (ed.). 1954. *The Grove Dictionary of Musical Instruments*, 5th ed., London.
Boalch, Donald H. 1956/1974. *Makers of the Harpsichord and Clavichord 1440–1840*, 1st and 2nd eds. (3rd ed. pending), London.
Conner, Patrick (ed.). 1983. *The Inspiration of Egypt: Its Influence on British Artists, Travellers and Designers, 1700–1900* (Exhibition Catalogue, Brighton Museum, 7 May–17 July, 1983, and Manchester City Art Gallery, 4 August–17 September, 1983), Brighton.
Ehrenhofer, Walter E. 1914. 'Auffindung einer Flaschenorgel', in *Zeitschrift für Instrumentenbau* 34.
Farrington, Frank. 1969. 'Dissection of a serpent', in *Galpin Society Journal*, XXII.
Fox, David H. 1992. *Robert Hope-Jones*, Virginia.
Fox and Sons. 1927. *Catalogue of the Contents of the Mansion, Brownsea Castle, Brownsea Island, Poole Harbour, Dorset*, 13–23 June, Bournemouth.
Halfpenny, Eric. 1964. 'Lament for Fusedale Tecil', in *Galpin Society Journal*, XVII.
Hampton and Sons. 1913. *Catalogue of the Well-known and Interesting Collection of Antique Furniture and Objets d'Art Formed by the late Sir Lawrence Alma-Tadema, O.M., R.A.*, 9 June, London.
Hands, R.A. 1967. 'A Scientific approach to the clavichord', in *Galpin Society Journal*, XX.
James, Philip. 1970. *Early Keyboard Instruments: From their Beginnings to the Year 1820* (1st ed. 1930), London.
Knight, Frank and Rutley. 1926. *A Catalogue of Rare English Furniture and Works of Art Removed from Cheshire*, 3–4 June, London.
Langwill, Lyndesay G. 1977. *An Index of Musical Wind-Instrument Makers*, 5th ed., Edinburgh.
The Liverpolitan. 1937. 'Liverpool's Historical Treasures', in *The Liverpolitan*, August.
Mould, Charles. 1974. 'The Broadwood Books: 2', in *The English Harpsichord Magazine*, Vol.1, 2, April.
Paris Universal International Exhibition. 1878. *Official Catalogue of the British Section, Part 1*, London.

Remnant, Mary. 1978. *Musical Instruments of the West*, London.

R & D catalogue 1. Undated. *The Rushworth and Dreaper Permanent Collection of Antique Musical Instruments*, Liverpool.

R & D catalogue 2. Undated. *The Rushworth and Dreaper Collection of Antique Musical Instruments and Historical Manuscripts*, Liverpool.

Russell, Raymond. 1959/1973. *The Harpsichord and Clavichord* (1st and 2nd eds.), London.

Sayer, Michael. 1981. 'New Light on Hope-Jones', in *The Organ* 235, January.

Schindler, Jurgen-Peter. Undated. 'Ganz ruiniert und theilweise bestholen', unprovenanced photocopy of article, in possession of Editor.

Spiegl, Fritz. 1972. 'Pipes, Pedals and Puff', in *Cheshire Life*, October.

Strack, Wolfgang. 1977. 'Christian Gottleb Hubert, Hochfürstlich Ansbach-Bayreuthischer Hof-, Orgel-und Instrumentenmacher' in *Das Musikinstrument* XXVI, December.

Strack, Wolfgang. 1979. 'Christian Gottlob Hubert and his Instruments', in *Galpin Society Journal* XXXII.

Taylor, Stainton de B. 1976. *Two Centuries of Music in Liverpool*, Liverpool.

Waterhouse, William. 1993. *The New Langwill Index. A Dictionary of Musical Wind-Instrument Makers and Inventors*, London.

Weston, Stephen. 1983. 'Improvements to the nine-keyed ophicleide', in *Galpin Society Journal*, XXXVI.

Weston, Stephen. 1989. 'Ophicleide Crooks', in *Galpin Society Journal*, XLII.

Wilson, Michael. 1968. *The English Chamber Organ : History and Development, 1650–1850*, Oxford.

Whittington-Egan, Richard. 1976. 'The Pipes of Pan and the Serpent', in *Liverpool Roundabout*, Liverpool.

Wraight, Denzil. 1992. Letter in *Early Music*, November.

Young, Philip T. 1978. 'Inventory of Instruments: J.H. Eichentopf, Poerschman, Sattler, A & H Grenser, Grundmann,' in *Galpin Society Journal*, XXXI.

Index

of Musical Instrument Makers and Retailers

Abromovicha, Ivana 116
Aeolian Company 156
Aeolian Organ and Music Co. 157
Aeolian, Weber Piano and Pianola Co. 157
Albertini and Sons, Carlo 110
Andrews and Co, Thomas 13
Anglo-American Zither Company 126
Audsley, William James and George Ashdown 36, 37, 38

Baffo, Joannes Antonius 2, 3
Baggaley, Cecil 101
Bainbridge, William 80
Bainbridge and Wood 80, 81, 82, 83
Ball Beavan 131
Banger, Josiah 76
Banks, James and Henry 134
Bates and Son, T. C. 160, 161
Bell and Crane Music Ltd 34, 35, 63
Bendon and Co., George 166, 167
Betts 143
Bontems 178
Bontems, Blaise 178
Boosey and Co. 90
Boosey and Hawkes 90
Bratya Grimm (Grimm Brothers) 115
Bremond, and Co., B.A. 172
Broadwood, John 12
Broadwood, John and Sons 6, 25, 28
Brown, A. 69
Browne, H. Justin 34
Buntebart, Gabriel 16
Busson, M. 65

Chickering and Sons 40
Clementi and Co. 76, 79, 118, 119
Clementi, Muzio 76

Collard and Collard 76
Collard, Frederick William 76
Corsby, John 131
Crane and Sons Ltd 34, 63
Cristofori, Bartolomeo 5

D'Almaine and Co. 74
Davis, David 76
Dodd, Edward 142
Dodd, John 142
Doherty, William 64
Doherty, W. and Co. 63, 64
Doherty Piano Company 64
Doherty Piano and Organ Company 64
Dolmetsch, Arnold 2, 3, 5, 40, 41, 87
Dreaper, William Henry and George Henry ix, 30, 36, 37
Dreaper and Son, William P. 30, 32

Eberle, Johann Ulrich 132
English Automatic Seraphone Company 163
Erat, Jacob and Sons 120, 122
Erat, James 120
Erat, John 120

Franciolini, Leopoldo 5
Freeman 75
Fuchs and Wollner 88
Fusedale, John 93, 94

Gaveau 43, 44
Gilbert 50
Goulding and D'Almaine 74
Grober, Johann 23
Grundmann, Jakob Friedrich 72, 73

Hansen, Karl 48
Hastrick 80
Hawkes and Son 90

Hemmings, George 148
Herrburger Brooks Ltd 42
Hill and Son, William 55
Hohner 35
Hope-Jones Organ Company Ltd 55
Hope-Jones, Robert 55, 56, 57
Hubert, Christian Gottlob 14
Hyde, Frederick Augustus 76

Jordan, James 77

Key, Thomas 77
Kirckman, Jacob 9, 11
Kirshaw, John 7
Klein Ltd, Dan 37
Krenke, George 20, 132
Kühlewein, Johann Samuel 52, 53

Lea, William 176
Leclerc 69
Lecoultre Frères 164
Lee, Frederick John 106
Light, Edward 119
Longman, John 76
Longman and Broderip 76

Maggs, John 92
Manderscheid, Nicolaus 46
Manning, Wilbur 64
Meinhold, T. 127
Melville Clark 154, 155
Menzenhauer 125
Merchel, Johann Friedrich 108
Metzler and Co. 78
Metzler, George 78
Metzler, G. and Co. 78
Metzler and Son 78
Metzler, Valentin 78
Miller, G. 76
Morris, Charles 66

Norman and Beard Ltd 55

Orsi, Romeo 100

Pace, Charles 98
Pace, Frederick 98
Paillard, Amedee 165
Paillard, C. and Co. 165
Paillard, E. and Co. 165
Paillard, Vaucher, Fils (PVF) 165, 170
Palmer, James 60
Perry, Thomas 138

Pesario 2
Phillips, William 158
Poerschman, Johann 73
Poggi, Francesco 2, 5
Polyphon Musikwerke 175, 176
Pollard, John 101
Potter, Henry and Co. 84

Reuge 178
Robertson and Co. 27
Robertson, James 96
Rogers, George and Sons 39
Rosenburger, Michael 23
Rushworth and Dreaper Ltd vi, viii, ix, x, 5, 6, 8, 11, 12, 13, 15, 17, 20, 23, 24, 32, 33, 41, 42, 43, 47, 48, 50, 52, 54, 69, 73, 74, 80, 81, 82, 88, 98, 100, 101, 108, 111, 119, 131, 132, 138, 139, 142, 144, 145, 148, 158, 161, 168, 171, 172
Ryalls and Jones Ltd 39

Samuels Ltd, D. 68
Schrader and Hartz 16
Sherlock, John Frank 64
Sherlock Manning 64
Shudi, Burkat 12
Skinner Company, the Ernest M. 157
Smith and Son, 156, 157
Snell and Co. 28, 29
Snetzler, John 49
Soprani, Paolo 68
Stansfield, Edward 136
Steck, George 156, 157
Stein, Johann Andreas 20

Thompson, J. Albert 62
Tixier, Pierre 144
Trayser and Co., Philip J. 60
Tremaine, Harry 157
Tremaine, William B. 157

Vuillaume, Jean-Baptiste 142

Walter, Anton 23
Ward, Cornelius 85
Ward, Richard J. 85, 102
Ward, Roger 85
Ward and Sons 85, 162
Wilkinson, William 138

Ziuzina, U. 116